The Prize

The Prize

Lance Lambert

LANCE LAMBERT MINISTRIES
Richmond, VA

ISBN 978-1-68389-091-1
www.lancelambert.org

Contents

Preface

Brethren, I count not myself yet to have laid hold: but one thing I do, forgetting the things which are behind, and stretching forward to the things which are before, I press on toward the goal unto the prize of the high calling of God in Christ Jesus. Philippians 3:7–14

In looking at the Christian walk as a race, we can often see obstacles that could prevent us from finishing well. How can we press on after Christ? There is a way. The obstacles of self, and sin, and the world do not have to prevent us from going on after Christ.

Let's seek the Lord's victorious way in this race together in these chapters and be encouraged to 'lay aside every weight, and the sin which doth so easily beset us' (Hebrews 12:1).

1.
The Goal and the Prize

Philippians 3:1–16

Finally, my brethren, rejoice in the Lord. To write the same things to you, to me indeed is not irksome, but for you it is safe. Beware of the dogs, beware of the evil workers, beware of the concision: for we are the circumcision, who worship by the Spirit of God, and glory in Christ Jesus, and have no confidence in the flesh: though I myself might have confidence even in the flesh: if any other man thinketh to have confidence in the flesh, I yet more:
circumcised the eighth day, of the stock of Israel, of the tribe of Benjamin, a Hebrew of Hebrews; as touching the law, a Pharisee; as touching zeal, persecuting the church; as touching the righteousness which is in the law, found blameless. Howbeit what things were gain to me, these have I counted loss for Christ. Yea verily, and I count all things to be loss for the excellency of the knowledge of Christ Jesus my Lord: for whom I suffered the loss of all things, and do count them but refuse, that I

may [win] gain Christ, and be found in him, not having a righteousness of mine own, even that which is of the law, but that which is through faith in Christ, the righteousness which is from God by faith: that I may know him, and the power of his resurrection, and the fellowship of his sufferings, becoming conformed unto his death; if by any means I may attain unto the resurrection from the dead. Not that I have already obtained, or am already made perfect: but I press on, if so be that I may lay hold on that for which also I was laid hold on by Christ Jesus. Brethren, I count not myself yet to have laid hold: but one thing I do, forgetting the things which are behind, and stretching forward to the things which are before, I press on toward the goal unto the prize of the high calling of God in Christ Jesus. Let us therefore, as many as are perfect, be thus minded: and if in anything ye are otherwise minded, this also shall God reveal unto you: only, whereunto we have attained, by that same rule let us walk.

Shall we pray?

Beloved Lord, we bow in Your presence to recognize that when it comes to the ministry of Your word, without You we can do nothing. Indeed, dear Lord, we know that apart from You we can do nothing in any way. But when it comes to Your word, there are many truths we can outline and many words we can use, and it can all be sound and good and Biblical. But unless You are here and unless You give that enabling grace and power to speak Your word and to hear Your word, there will be nothing that goes into eternity.

Lord, we want to be those in whom that eternal weight of glory is being worked. Therefore, beloved Lord, we come to You and praise You together that You have not left us to our own abilities or our own talents or our own energies. But You have provided us with an anointing in our Lord Jesus, made a living reality in the Person of the Holy Spirit. Into that anointing grace and power we stand by faith. We look to You, Lord, that you will manifest that anointing, both in the speaking of Your word and in the hearing of it, that out of this time there may come something for Yourself in every one of our lives and in our life together as Your people. We shall be very careful, Lord, to give You all the praise and all the glory for answering this our prayer, which we ask in the name of our Lord Jesus, the Messiah. Amen.

There are many extraordinary testimonies in the Bible. In fact, we could say that the Bible is a book of testimonies. But in my estimation there is no testimony as remarkable or as significant as this testimony of the apostle Paul contained in Philippians 3:12–14: "Not that I have already obtained, or am already made perfect: but I press on, if so be that I may lay hold on that for which also I was laid hold on by Christ Jesus. Brethren, I count not myself yet to have laid hold: but one thing I do, forgetting the things which are behind, and stretching forward to the things which are before, I press on toward the goal unto the prize of the high calling of God in Christ Jesus."

An Extraordinary Testimony

I want to look at this testimony of the apostle Paul and then as the Lord enables me, take up certain very practical and vitally important aspects of this testimony. The first thing I would like to say, not to be a Bible critic, is that this testimony raises very serious questions, even serious questions about the apostle Paul himself. Is he contradicting himself? Is he contradicting what he has been used by the Lord to convey to us again and again in the Roman letter, in the I and II Corinthian letters, and in other letters of his? It is quite amazing when you look at it.

For example, he says, "I count not myself yet to have laid hold." Well, where does that leave you and where does that leave me? This is not a slip of the tongue with the apostle Paul because he goes on to say, "Not that I have already obtained, or am already made perfect."

Now, we could fully understand him saying, "Not that I am already made perfect." But to say "I have not yet obtained," I think raises very serious questions. Then he says, "I count not myself yet to have laid hold." This man has had incredible experiences. He actually saw the Lord on the road to Damascus. It was not just a vision, but in that seeing of the Lord so much was later to come out in his understanding of the purpose of God, of the church of God, of the Christian life. So much came out of what he saw that day when Jesus said to him: "Saul, Saul, why do you persecute me?" The apostle Paul could easily have said, "I am not persecuting You, Lord; I am persecuting these people who are Your followers."

But from this amazing vision came a whole understanding that when you touch the simplest child of God, you touch the

Lord. When you despise the simplest member of the church of God, you despise the Lord. When you disregard or devalue some member of the body of Christ—whoever it is, if that one is saved by the grace of God and born of the Holy Spirit—you are actually devaluing the Lord Jesus. That vision was so amazing that the apostle had on the road to Damascus!

There are many other things too. He had already written the Roman letter, all sixteen chapters of it. He had already written the I and II Corinthian letters, the Galatian letter, the I and II Thessalonian letters, and the little letter to Philemon. I would have said that by normal Christian standards it looks as if he had laid hold on the Lord. If I take what he says, I would have said that if there is one person in the church who had laid hold on that for which he was laid hold on by Christ, it is the apostle Paul.

But he says, "I count not myself yet to have laid hold." Is he being falsely modest? Is he doing that sham thing that we find so prevalent among Christians: "Oh, I am nothing; I am nothing"? If you go around and say so and so is nothing, you are in for trouble; they get very angry. But they say, "I am nothing; I am nothing at all." Do not treat them on their own evaluation or they will get very angry with you.

Was it a false modesty in the apostle Paul when he said, "I count not myself yet to have laid hold"? Was he just saying, "I know very well that you all know I have laid hold. You have only got to read my letters and you can see very well how far I have gotten, how I have taken hold of the Lord, and the experiences I have had. Do you know that I have even been caught up to the third heaven?"

"I have been caught up to the third heaven and I have heard things that are not even lawful to utter," he could say if he was here. In many Christian circles you would write a book on it or travel the platforms of the world saying, "What I heard in the third heaven," or "What I saw in the third heaven." But the apostle Paul, who had been caught up to the third heaven, would not even tell us what he saw and what he heard there. He said, "It is not lawful to mention it." This is incredible when you think of his testimony—shipwrecked and left for dead a number of times. Yet he says, "I do not consider myself yet to have laid hold. I have not already obtained."

What is he talking about? Is he talking about salvation? But surely this apostle is the one who told us that the free gift of God is eternal life in Christ Jesus our Lord. What does he mean, "I have not already obtained"? Does he mean that he is not sure that he is saved? That is what I meant when I said at the beginning: This testimony raises serious questions. Had Paul just had a bad night when he wrote this letter? Maybe it is one of those testimonies he gave to the Corinthians when he wrote the second letter and said: "I did have a bad time about that first letter I wrote to you."

I find this very interesting. If there is one person in the church whom we would have considered to have obtained, whom we would have considered at least coming near to being perfected in the Lord, whom we would have considered to have laid hold on that for which Christ laid hold on him, I would have thought it would be the apostle Paul.

There are some more, I think, even more serious questions in this testimony. What does he mean, "That I may know Him"? Surely he does know Him. It is one thing to say, "I count all things but loss for the excellency of the knowledge of Christ Jesus my

Lord." We understand that. He is counting all things loss for this excellency of the knowledge of Christ Jesus his Lord. But then he goes on to say "That I may know Him," as if he does not really know the Lord. He does not say, "That I may know about Him, but that I may know Him." But surely he knows the Lord. Surely he already knows the Lord in a very deep way.

There is an even more serious question. He says, "That I may win Christ." What is he talking about? Is he a Catholic? Maybe it was not Peter who founded the Catholic Church; maybe it was Paul. Listen again: "That I may win Christ" (v. 8). What is he talking about? The Lord Jesus is God's unspeakable gift to us. He is God's unspeakable gift to sinners and that gift to us is a gift of grace. It is unconditional. What does he mean, "That I may win Christ"? There is no getting out of this. It is not just some bad translation of the Greek. It does not matter how you put it— gain Christ, win Christ—it is the same thing. He is giving this idea of winning Christ. Isn't Christ already Paul's?

He qualifies this in a most interesting way. He says, "That I may win Christ, and be found in Him, not having a righteousness of mine own, even that which is of the law." In other words, this winning of Christ is not of works. Did you hear that? He is not preaching a form of Catholicism. He said, "That I may be found in Him, not having a righteousness which is of the law, but that which is through faith in Christ, the righteousness which is from God by faith."

So this winning of Christ is solidly based upon the justifying work of the Lord Jesus. It is solidly based in the grace of God. Then, what is he talking about, "That I may win Christ"?

I have a further problem, which is in verse 11: "That I may attain unto the resurrection from the dead." I do not know what the apostle Paul is talking about. Everybody will come to the resurrection of the dead, even the ungodly and the unsaved. They will all stand before the great white throne of judgment. So what is he talking about? It is even more interesting in the Greek. It is literally: "That I may attain unto the out-resurrection from among the dead." It is a very especial resurrection that he is talking about.

I do not know if I am confusing you more than you are already confused. Even though we read this kind of thing, we do not take it so seriously. We read through it all, and of course, "win Christ," means He is God's unspeakable gift to us by grace. We do not put too much on winning and gaining and attaining unto the resurrection. Maybe we think that perhaps it is just a little bit of Jewish exaggeration on the part of Paul. We do not get stuck on that kind of thing. We just move over it quickly. But I say this raises serious questions. What does it all signify?

It is clearly very important and very significant because the apostle says, "Forgetting the things which are behind, and stretching forward to the things which are before, I press on toward the goal unto the prize of the high calling of God in Christ Jesus."

The On-High Calling of God

We have something here of tremendous significance and tremendous gravity. It means that every child of God has a calling and this calling has something to do with a goal. Your salvation is not in itself the goal. Your salvation is not an end in itself. Your salvation is a glorious and powerful means by which you are once again in the calling of God. We fell short of the glory of God by sin. Being saved by the grace of God, we are called by Him. So all I want to do is just to underline this matter.

First of all, in verse 14, there are two little words: *goal* and *prize*. A prize is won; a goal is reached.

The second thing I want to talk about is the prize of the high calling of God in Christ Jesus. "Toward the goal unto the prize of the high calling of God in Christ Jesus."

"Forgetting the things that are behind." This does not mean that you forget the principles of your salvation. It does not mean that you forget the foundation upon which you stand. It does not mean that you treat as kindergarten the good news concerning God's Son. But it does mean that you are not stuck there. Forgetting the things which are behind, you press on or you stretch forward to the things which are before. What are the things which are before? A goal and a prize.

First of all, it is a high calling of God. This is God's calling. This is not a human calling; it is not a church calling; it is not something to do merely with theology. It is a divine calling.

The Spirit of Wisdom and Revelation

In Ephesians 1:18 it says, "Having the eyes of your heart enlightened, that ye may know what is the hope of his calling." Do you know what the hope of His calling is? Could you put it in a sentence? If you had to write an essay or fill a whole page, you have not seen it. You should be able to put in a few sentences, actually in one sentence, what is the hope of His calling. This is so important.

When the apostle Paul was dictating this letter to this dear person, whoever it was, who was like a secretary to him writing it out in full, they must have stopped at one point. (This is how my fevered imagination works.) Did they have prayer together? It is quite possible he said, "This is so important, let's have a word of prayer." Then maybe the secretary said, "Don't you think you should tell them what we prayed?" "Well," the apostle may have said, "is it quite in the line of what we are trying to say to the folks at Ephesus?" Then I suppose he thought: "I am so afraid this Ephesian letter will just be material for theological seminaries or material merely for sermons. Let's tell them what we are praying."

"We are praying that the God and Father of our Lord Jesus the Messiah may grant to you a spirit of wisdom and revelation." Wisdom what to do with knowledge. It is not just knowledge but wisdom—how it applies to your life, what to do with it in your life.

Revelation is illumination. It is when the Holy Spirit shines into our heart and something we know as a doctrine suddenly becomes reality to us. It changes our whole life. Theology has never changed anybody's life. It is very necessary. Do not despise theology. It is necessary to keep us from error and so much else. But theology never changed a person's life. It is when the eyes of our hearts are enlightened that something happens. Suddenly we see what it is all about. To begin with, if it follows my own experience, again and again you cannot even explain it to somebody else. You are tongue-tied. You know exactly what it is and yet you cannot, as you say in American English, verbalize it. We say in proper English that you cannot articulate it.

This is an amazing thing, the very first thing the apostle Paul says, "The eyes of your heart being enlightened, that you may know, not about, but you may know directly, intimately, clearly, what is the hope of His calling." Are you a child of God? Do you know what the hope of His calling is? I think this is tremendous.

In Romans 8:28 it says, "And we know that to them that love God all things work together for good, even to them that are called according to his purpose." We often quote this part of the Scripture: "All things work together for good to them that love God." But we do not always take in this part: "who are called according to His purpose."

When we got saved, we hardly realized it but we were called according to a purpose. Most of us had no idea when we were saved, what God had saved us for. All we knew was that God had saved us. He had forgiven our sin; He had cleansed us; He brought us to a new birth. We did not realize that we were saved according to His purpose, called according to His purpose.

In II Timothy 1:9 it says, "Who saved us, and called us with a holy calling, not according to our works, but according to his own purpose and grace, which was given us in Christ Jesus before times eternal." This simply means that you were given this calling before times eternal. It is not just something to do with your little life now, although by the grace of God you have come into it.

There is Grace and Power to Reach God's Goal

It says, "He has saved us and called us." Once you are saved, you are called. Your salvation is a means to bring you into the calling of God and then to the goal of God. And within your salvation is everything you need to reach God's goal.

Of course, we are all adept at excuses. We all say, "Well, if you knew my circumstances, you would understand. I am sure the Lord understands I have very difficult parents. I have very difficult children. I have a very difficult husband. I have a very difficult wife. I have a very difficult employee. I have a very difficult employer." We are so clever about this. "Oh, if you knew my circumstances, you would understand. I am excused for being very slow on this whole matter because I have very unusual circumstances." But there is no excuse because if you have unusual circumstances, you have unusual grace. If you have difficult relatives, you are given all the power of the Holy Spirit commensurate with the difficulty you have with relatives. If you have difficulties at work you have both the grace and power that is sufficient for all those problems. So we are actually without excuse.

God has not suddenly woken up to the fact that you are an especial case. "Well, if I had known this before, I would never have saved them in the first place. They are quite clearly an especial case. They have problems that others do not have. They have a background the others do not have. They have inherited temperaments that the others do not have. They have a genetic history that the others do not seem to have. If I had only known this to begin with I might have passed over so and so."

No, no, no. God knew you in your mother's womb. He knows more about your mother than you ever knew about your mother. He knows more about your grandmother, and your grandfather, and your great-grandmother. Your whole genetic history is an open book as far as God is concerned. When He saved you,

He said, "This person is going to be a difficulty, and this person is going to have a lot of problems. But I am making available grace for the problems and power for the difficulties. They will have to discover that grace and that power, and by so doing they will come to the goal, to the prize of the high calling of God in Christ Jesus. So this is tremendous when you begin to look at it like this.

In Ephesians 4:1 the apostle says, "I beseech you to walk worthily of the calling wherewith ye were called." In other words, we cannot be worthy in ourselves but we can walk worthily. We can walk worthily of the calling wherewith we are called. Do not treat it lightly. Do not despise the calling with which you are called. Walk worthily of the calling. You cannot be worthy in yourself. None of us can. I cannot be; you cannot be, but we can walk in a worthy manner. We may not understand it all but at least we know this is tremendous, that God has called us. Now I am a child of God. I have been called by the Lord into this.

The High Calling is in Christ Jesus

Here is the second thing. This high calling of God is in Christ Jesus. The high calling of God on your life is something to do with the Lord Jesus. Get it! It is something to do with the Lord Jesus. That is why it is the hope of His calling. God's whole eternal purpose is centered in the Lord Jesus, and this high calling of God is in Him.

What does it mean? It means that God has called you to share His glory, to share His life, the life of Christ, to share the throne of Christ, and to share the destiny of Christ. Of course, there is a glory of the Lord Jesus that is absolutely unique. In that sense, you and I cannot share it. But we are called to share the life and the destiny of the Lord Jesus. This high calling of God is in Christ.

The Upward Calling

Then there is another marvelous thing here. In the Greek this high calling is an upward calling. Some people have translated this the on-high calling of God in Christ Jesus. But the idea is that God is calling us up, out of the things that bind us, out of the things that are like tentacles around us. It is an upward calling of God in Christ Jesus—the goal and the prize.

How do you explain this goal, this prize? This is how I explain it, at least how it has come to me in my understanding. You receive the Lord Jesus as Savior. You receive Him as Redeemer. You receive Him as Deliverer. You receive Him as Life. You receive Him in all these ways, but you win Him as Bridegroom. And the winning of the Lord Jesus as Bridegroom is based in the grace of God. It is not that you are good, that it is all your own zeal and devotion and energy. It is that by the grace that is given to you in the Lord Jesus and because of the power of the Holy Spirit that is yours in the Lord Jesus, you win Him as Bridegroom.

What does it mean to lay hold on Him? This can just be a wonderful sermon but the practical thing is whether you can lay hold on that for which Christ has laid hold on you. Are you? My experience with so many Christians is that they are not laying hold on that for which they were laid hold on by Christ. When it comes down to it, it is as simple as that.

The Bible Ends with a City and a Bride

When you come to the last chapters of the Bible with the New Jerusalem, the holy city as it is called, the bride, the wife of the Lamb, these are extraordinary terms. A capital city and a bride, the wife of the Lamb, are two totally disparate ideas or concepts. A capital city is the center of administration, the center of government, the center where policies are defined and followed through and fulfilled.

Think of Washington for just a moment. That is where all the government of a whole nation is centered. And that is the way the Bible ends, with a capital city. It speaks of government, it speaks of a throne, it speaks of rule and reigning, it speaks of a kingdom, if you like, it speaks of an empire, it speaks of all this administration. And those who are part of this city are evidently going to reign with Christ forever and ever. They have come to the throne. They are sharing the throne with the Lord Jesus.

Then you have another picture, and that is the bride, the wife of the Lamb. In the Bible that always speaks of intimacy, of sensitivity, of union and communion. You have heard me say many times that I have gone all over the world and never, ever has anyone anywhere introduced his wife to me as his capital city—"Here is my capital city." Sometimes the wife has all the money but he still does not say, "Here is my capital city." Sometimes the wife runs everything, but I have never heard any husband say, "Here is my capital city." Some of them look like capital cities I might add, but never have I ever been introduced to a wife as his capital city because these two concepts are so different. They do not belong together normally.

What then is the Lord saying? He is simply saying that He does not want an eternal bureaucracy. He does not want a kind of impersonal civil service able to administer His will without compassion, without feeling, without sensitivity. We all know what it is like to be in the hands sometimes of such people. He wants a government that is in union and communion with Him, that has an intimacy with him, that is sensitive to Him, that has His character.

There is one very interesting thing about this that is true of both of these concepts that are brought together in one, and it is very, very simple. You cannot be part of a civil service unless first, you have had some years behind you, and secondly, you have had training, education, and discipline. Isn't that so?

Suddenly we discover that this city we always sing about, treading the streets of gold and going through the pearly gates, is not just any believer. It is not just babes in Christ, but it is those who have grown in the Lord. They have gone through training and education by the Spirit of God. They have known a discipline. They have learned how to discern the mind and heart of God and how to stand with Him for its fulfillment.

And the bride cannot be a baby. There are such things. In the old days in a royal family there was someone who was only two years of age who was actually married, but of course, it was not a marriage. There has to be a minimal maturity. It is not this idea that somehow or other the Lord can just get anyone there, and once He has you there He will sort of wave a kind of wand over you and suddenly you grow up. It does not happen that way. It takes time, it takes pressure, it takes decision on your part.

The Lord does not want a bride with Him in the ages to come who is there because she wants to escape hell, she is there because she wants to get a bit of glory, she is there because she is interested in herself. She is there because she loves Him. She is there because she has laid down her life and followed Him in His footsteps.

Pressing Toward the Goal

I want to make a few comments on Paul's words: "I press on toward the goal." Here is a man who has seen something so tremendous, so eternally significant, so glorious that he can never be the same again. It is not just theology. It is not even just truths. It is not even a concept. He has seen something in the Lord.

When you do not have much experience and very little knowledge of the subject, you can throw your weight around. Very often, in universities you get first and second year undergraduates who know it all. And when they are out, they will tell everybody else: "This is this, that is that, and this is the other." But if you speak to the professor he says, "Well, it could be this, and it could be that, and it could be that. I think it is this." Why is the two-year undergraduate so dogmatic and the professor who has been in the business for years and years is so "undogmatic"? It is because the professor knows a good deal more than the two-year undergraduate.

There are Christians who know it all. They give you the impression: "Come to me; I know it all. I have the Holy Spirit. I have had an experience of the Holy Spirit. I have had an experience of the Lord Jesus." Yes, you have. You have the Holy Spirit trapped in you in a straight jacket. You have the Lord Jesus in you in a straight jacket. It is an altogether different thing when the Holy Spirit gets you. Then you are immersed in the Holy Spirit. As Margaret Barber put it: "You are anchored to infinity." Something tremendous has happened. Instead of getting it all in your head, suddenly you are introduced to the infinity of God. Now you know there are unsearchable riches. That means you can never come to an end of them. Now you know there is a fathomless, exhaustless fulness. You can never plumb its depths completely. You come into such an experience of the Lord, of His greatness that you can never be the same again.

Abraham

When the God of glory appeared to our father Abraham, he was never the same again (see Acts 7). He was not some uneducated illiterate but an aristocrat in Ur of the Chaldees. The family was in the idol making business, very lucrative. It was a business, indeed, in the Babel complex of cities. But when the God of glory appeared to Abraham, he went out not knowing where he went. Something so tremendous happened that he was spoiled for anything less than God's best and God's highest. He could never again be satisfied with Ur of the Chaldees. He could never again be satisfied with his idol business. He could not even be interested anymore merely in making money. He went out not knowing where he went. He was led step by step all the way through.

Paul had the same experience. Something so took him that the more he knew the Lord, the more he knew there was to know. And the realization came to him how little he really knew. That is the explanation of this extraordinary testimony because he saw so much he could only say, "I do not count myself yet to have laid hold. There is so much more to take hold of. I have not already obtained or already made perfect."

Moses

I think of Moses, grandson of Pharaoh, who was brought up in the royal house with a royal education. He had everything that could be the very best and the very highest in the greatest empire of the day. And God took Moses out into a desert and he looked after smelly sheep and goats, and camels that are even more smelly than sheep and goats. For forty years he looked after them. Forty years, not four years; forty years, not fourteen years; forty years! For most of us that is a lifetime. We are ready to retire after that. Forty years and then God appeared to him. And God appeared to him in such a way that it was quite remarkable. It was in a little, old, thorn bush; stupid really. Can anyone believe that God could get into a thorn bush? It was not a big tree, but something low down, and the Lord spoke up at Moses and said, "Do not come any nearer. Take the shoes from off your feet; the ground whereon you stand is holy." What an extraordinary thing! The bush burned with fire and the bush was not consumed. Is it any wonder that a year or two later Moses said, "Show me Your glory?" He had been caught by something. It is as simple as that. He was caught by a vision of the Lord. Once he was caught there was no escape. He could not go back; he could not get out of it. All he could say was, "Lord, show me Your glory." And the Lord said, "That is all right; I will hide you in the cleft of the rock. I will pass by and you shall see My glory, but you will only see My backside, as it were."

Jacob

Think of dear Jacob. What a mess he was! He was a very gifted young man. People always speak of Jacob as if he were the effeminate twin, as if he were spineless and anemic. Poor thing, he was left at home. He was a kind of interior designer type. You can only feel a bit sorry for the poor fellow. His brother was the real outdoor type. He was a wonderful fellow, broad and strong and hairy, a sort of man's man. But this poor old Jacob is thought to be a mother's boy, which was not even true, not even a little true.

Jacob had no answer to the strength of his nature. It was incredible. He deceived his old father; he had deceived his twin brother. You know the story. But when God met with him, he said, "I have seen the face of God and I have lived." There is no one you would think would be more burnt up by seeing the Lord than old twisted Jacob. But he said, "I saw the face of God and I have lived." And he was never the same again.

Pharaoh himself bowed down before him. It is amazing. The last picture we have of Jacob is of him leaning on his staff or on his bedpost (we are not quite sure which it is in the Hebrew) and worshiping. He was never a worshiper; he was a bargainer. He was always out for a good deal, a smart deal. The man had become a worshiper, and he blessed Joseph's two sons. He was not someone one who could bless anybody. He stole from everybody. He stole the birthright from his twin brother. He stole the blessing of his twin brother from his father. But at the end he blessed others.

You see this vision of the Lord everywhere, no matter where you turn. These servants of God with all their failings, all their problems, and all their weaknesses had been caught by a vision of the Lord that had changed the course of their lives. They could never be the same again. They could not go back; they could not get out of it. They could only press on.

David

King David—oh, what a mess he got into with Bathsheba. By general standards you would have expected for his life to have been taken by the Lord for such a crime. But David, if we read his Psalms, thirsted for the Lord. He hungered for the Lord. And in the end, the amazing thing is that his very sin drove him to the Lord. Perhaps one of the most remarkable things I find in the Bible (and this is no excuse for sin by the way) is that Bathsheba became the mother of Solomon and Nathan, both of them in the Messianic line. Once confessed, David could never be the same again.

"When you said to me, "Seek ye my face, my heart said unto You, Your face, Lord, will I seek…I had fainted unless I had believed to see the goodness of the Lord in the land of the living" (See Psalm 27:8, 13). The man was caught; there was no escape. He could not get away.

Isaiah

One of the greatest and most prophetic ministries in the Bible is Isaiah. When the Lord first really met Isaiah, it was at the point of great depression when King Uzziah had died under judgment as a leper. When Isaiah saw the Lord high and lifted up and his train filling the temple, he was never the same again. Out of it came a whole ministry that is one of the greatest ministries in the old covenant. We call him the great evangelical prophet.

Hunger and Thirst After Righteousness

Do you know that one of the greatest blessings you and I can have is the blessedness of hunger and thirst? Jesus said in Matthew 5:6: "Blessed are those who hunger and thirst after righteousness, for they shall be filled."

Of course, it is true that our Lord Jesus said, "I am the bread of life. He that eateth of me and drinketh my blood shall never hunger or thirst again." It is absolutely true. He said that in John 6, and He said it to the woman at the well of Samaria in John 4. But the fact still remains that hunger and thirst are a tremendous blessing.

When a child of God has no hunger and no thirst, it means they are complacent, comfortable. What does it mean you will never hunger again, you will never thirst again? It surely means that your hunger will not be met anywhere outside of Christ. You will find your hunger met in the Lord Jesus. You will find your thirst met in the Lord Jesus.

But dear brothers and sisters, isn't it a curse when there is no hunger and no thirst? This apostle is a man who is hungry for the Lord, thirsty for the Lord. He knows the Lord can meet him. He knows the Lord is his only answer. He is prepared to count everything loss that he may really know this Lord.

It is a great tragedy when our assemblies and fellowships are filled with complacent, affluent, and comfortable people. We fall into a routine. There is no disturbing of us. Hunger is a very disturbing thing; so is thirst.

It is amazing to me that at the end of his life Paul was still hungry for the Lord and still thirsty for the Lord, still seeking out the Lord, still stretching forward to the Lord. Where does this leave me? And where does it leave you? I do not know of a single servant of God whom the Lord has ever used in the history of the church who has not had this same character as the apostle Paul.

"I press on toward the goal unto the prize of the high calling of God in Christ Jesus." May the Lord touch your heart. If you are one of those who has gotten complacent and comfortable, Laodicean really—we have the Lord's Table, we have the prayer meetings, we have the Bible study, we have the gospel meeting, we have everything—but we do not even know that the Lord is outside, knocking on the door and saying, "If any man hear My voice and open the door I will come in and will sup with him and he with me." If you are in that condition, open the door and He will come in and sup with you and you with Him.

Shall we pray:

Beloved Lord, You know everyone of us. We are like an open book as far as You are concerned. Beloved Lord, You know our hearts. We pray that You will stir them, that You will touch them by Your Spirit. Lord, if we have somehow got to a place where we are just comfortable, disturb us. Bring about within our spirit and heart a hunger for You, a thirst for You. As the Psalmist said, "My heart and my soul cry out for the living God." Do it, Lord, for Your name's sake, we ask. Amen

2.
Reaching the Goal and Obtaining the Prize

Philippians 3:7–14

Howbeit what things were gain to me, these have I counted loss for Christ. Yea verily, and I count all things to be loss for the excellency of the knowledge of Christ Jesus my Lord: for whom I suffered the loss of all things, and do count them but refuse, that I may gain [win] Christ, and be found in him, not having a righteousness of mine own, even that which is of the law, but that which is through faith in Christ, the righteousness which is from God by faith:

that I may know him, and the power of his resurrection, and the fellowship of his sufferings, becoming conformed unto his death; if by any means I may attain unto the resurrection from the dead. Not that I have already obtained, or am already made perfect: but I press on, if so be that I may lay hold on that for which also I was laid hold on by Christ Jesus. Brethren, I count not myself yet to have laid hold: but one thing I do, forgetting the things which are behind, and stretching

forward to the things which are before, I press on toward the goal unto the prize of the high calling of God in Christ Jesus

Revelation 3:16–22

So because thou art lukewarm, and neither hot nor cold, I will spew thee out of my mouth. Because thou sayest, I am rich, and have gotten riches, and have need of nothing; and knowest not that thou art the wretched one and miserable and poor and blind and naked: I counsel thee to buy of me gold refined by fire, that thou mayest become rich; and white garments, that thou mayest clothe thyself, and that the shame of thy nakedness be not made manifest; and eyesalve to anoint thine eyes, that thou mayest see. As many as I love, I reprove and chasten: be zealous therefore, and repent. Behold, I stand at the door and knock: if any man hear my voice and open the door, I will come in to him, and will sup with him, and he with me. He that overcometh, I will give to him to sit down with me in my throne, as I also overcame, and sat down with my Father in his throne. He that hath an ear, let him hear what the Spirit saith to the churches.

Shall we pray?

Beloved Lord, we are so thankful that we are gathered here in Your presence. We are glad, Lord, that we have been able freely to worship You. As we come to the ministry of Your word, we just want to recognize that without You we can do nothing that will go into eternity. But Lord, You have provided us with an anointing, a powerful anointing, an anointing of grace and power that will enable us to speak Your word and to hear Your word. We stand by faith into that anointing, won for us by our Lord Jesus on the cross and made such a living reality by the Holy Spirit to each one of us. Let that anointing be upon this whole meeting, Lord, and grant that the eyes of our heart being enlightened we might come to know what is the hope of the calling of our Lord Jesus. We ask it in His name. Amen.

This is an extraordinary testimony that we have here of the apostle Paul. The Bible is full of testimonies of all kinds. Everywhere you turn you find testimonies to the grace and to the power of God, to His holiness and to His justice. But of all the testimonies in the Bible I think this one of the apostle Paul's, contained in the Philippian letter is one of the most remarkable testimonies in all the sixty-six books of the Bible.

We have been singing this song: Give Us Vision, and that is precisely what happened to the apostle. But it was not just a physical vision of the risen Christ that he could talk about. I do not despise such visions, but he saw far more than the Lord Jesus, physically. He saw in the Lord Jesus everything that later he expounds in his letters.

It all began on that road to Damascus when the Lord Jesus Himself broke into the consciousness of this man who was obsessed with liquidating Messianic believers, Christians as they were later called. I find it quite remarkable that the apostle was inflamed by a vision of the greatness of the infinity of the Lord. So tremendous is this vision that he counted everything but loss. Here is a man born of the stock of Israel, a Hebrew of the Hebrews, born of the tribe of Benjamin. We who are Jewish are very proud of being Jewish. You can never de-Judaize us. We cannot help it. We are very proud. And the apostle was an example of enormous pride in his history, in his pedigree. Indeed, on three occasions Paul said, "I am a Jew"; not "I was a Jew," but "I am a Jew."

Paul says that he counts it all but refuse. The riches in the Lord Jesus are so tremendous, so fathomless. The fulness that was his in the Lord Jesus and the amazing call that had come from on high to him to press on, to come to the goal, to obtain the prize of the high calling of God in the Messiah, Jesus, that he considered everything else but refuse. In the light of what lies ahead, it is worthless, he says. If it becomes a means of holding us back, if it becomes a straightjacket into which we are found, if it becomes something that robs us of the power of the Lord and the grace of the Lord, it is all refuse.

He speaks about the excellency of the knowledge of Christ Jesus, the Lord. It is almost as if what he sees has somehow made him realize how much more there is to see. Somehow the knowledge that he has of the Lord has only inflamed him with an understanding that there is far more to know of the Lord than he has yet come to know. It is as if he feels that in experiencing what he has experienced of the Lord, there is far, far more ahead. So he says, "Forgetting the things which are behind and stretching forward to the things which are before, I press on toward the goal."

There is something incredibly attractive about a servant of God who has seen something of the infinity of God. And there is something incredibly dry about those who can manage to box God into certain statements, if you know what I mean.

I always remember Theodore Austin Sparks. Whatever faults and weaknesses he may have had, there is one thing that I can say and testify from my heart. I never heard him that I did not go away with a sense of the greatness of the Lord. I do not know how many times I heard him but I never ever heard him that I was not humbled by the infinity of the Lord, the greatness of the Lord. That is somehow so attractive. It captures us; it inflames us; it creates in us a hunger.

I remember the first time I met those two old missionaries who lived in Port Said. (I don't wish to be rude because they probably are in some way hearing what I am saying.) They were little old gray ladies, withered like prunes. You would pass them by on the street and not think twice about either of them. I will never forget when I was in their apartment in Port Said, and as I listened to them I realized I touched people who knew the Lord in a way that I did not know the Lord. Their knowledge of the Lord was not something that pulverized me. It was something that created in me a hunger and a thirst.

I remember on one occasion going out and walking up and down the great moor of the harbor on Port Said out into the sea, weeping. Here I was, someone who knew so much (I thought), who understood my Bible and had memorized so much of it, and now I felt as if I was an ignoramus with these people I had met. Yet they did not stuff it down me, if you know what I mean. They did not somehow beat me over the head with Scripture after Scripture. It was their very life, their prayer life, their very manner of living, something about them that inflamed me.

This is the thing we find with this apostle. Somehow or other he transmits something that makes us feel as if we do not know where we are. How little we really know of the Lord, how little we really have experienced of the Lord. Is it any wonder that he says,

"I press on toward the goal unto the prize of the high calling of God in Christ Jesus?"

This testimony, as recorded here in the Philippian letter, raises some very serious questions. What does the apostle Paul mean when he says, "That I may win Christ"? Christ is God's unspeakable gift to us. We do not win Him. What does he mean? Is it a slip of the tongue? Is it some mistake that got into the Bible?

"That I may gain Christ." Perhaps he meant, "That I may experience the Lord more deeply." But he says, "That I may win Christ." There is no way that you can translate this word in any other way. "That I may gain Christ. That I may win Christ." What does he mean?

What does he mean, "If by any means I may obtain unto the out-resurrection from among the dead"? What is he talking about?

We all know that there is a resurrection of the dead. We all know that for believers there is a first resurrection. But what is this out-resurrection from among the dead? What is it that he attains to?

We have serious questions. A prize is won; a goal is reached. As I understand it the Lord Jesus is given to us as Savior. He is given to us as Redeemer. He is given to us as Life. He is given to us as Lord. But we win Him as Bridegroom. That is the prize. That is the tremendous goal that is before every believer.

It is a tragedy that has befallen us as Christians, that somehow or other we think salvation is the end when it is only the beginning, when we think that salvation is an end in itself, when it is only a means to an end. Once you are saved, once you are born of God, then you hear, as it were, the calling, the upward calling of God in Christ Jesus. It is a calling to us, by the grace of

God and the power of God, to reach the goal, to obtain the prize of this upward calling of God in Christ Jesus.

For What Did the Lord Lay Hold of Us?

In Philippian 3:12 it says, "Not that I have already obtained, or am already made perfect: but I press on, if so be that I may lay hold on that for which also I was laid hold on by Christ Jesus."

I want to underline this little phrase here: "That for which also I was laid hold on by Christ Jesus." This is a most significant phrase. The Lord Jesus has laid hold of me; the Lord Jesus has laid hold of you. The word in Greek is a very strong word: apprehended, arrested. The Lord has arrested you. The Lord has apprehended you. The Lord has laid hold on you. Certainly it was so with the apostle Paul on that road to Damascus. He had no idea what was going to happen to him on that road to Damascus, but the Lord certainly laid hold on him.

"Laid hold on by Christ Jesus." If you are a child of God, even if you went forward and signed a decision form at some great crusade, it still was the Lord who laid hold on you. Maybe you thought you made a decision for the Lord, only to discover, if you have gone on with the Lord, that He took hold on you. He knew you from your mother's womb. He knows all your history. There is nothing about your life that is not an open book to the Lord, not a single thing. Everything that goes to make you what you are, to have produced the kind of personality you have is an open book to the Lord. He knows you. He knew you before you were even born. And the amazing thing is that in some incredible way, at some point in our life, whether it was when we were younger by the grace of God or when we were older, the Lord laid hold on us.

For what did the Lord lay hold on us? If I asked the question: "Why did the Lord lay hold on us?" That is a very good question. I have moved among believing people now ever since I was saved at the early age of thirteen, and I must say I sometimes wonder why the Lord ever saved the people He saved. I know that sounds a terrible thing to say. It is a very unloving thing to say, a very critical thing to say. But then, I am amazed that the Lord saved me. I have been nothing but trouble to the Lord. I do not know about you, but I know I have given the Lord so much trouble, endless trouble—murmuring, quarreling, and questioning. Sometimes the Lord has had to put a sort of spiritual explosion behind me to blow me forward now and again. This is the only way the Lord has to get us moving.

Why do I treat the Lord like this? Why do I have these arguments with the Lord? When the Lord shows us what His will is, why do we question it? It is very strange. I think it is because somehow deep within our hearts we are not quite sure that He really does love us. We fear that He wants to exploit us. He wants to use us. We are mere cannon fodder. We are merely a kind of impersonal mass of human beings that He wants to save, like trophies. He is like some old bewhiskered hunter who goes around his mansion and shows you all these heads. I shot that one in Uganda. That head I shot in Kenya. Ah, this one I shot in Bengal in India. It is the idea that we are all sort of trophies that the Lord has but He is not really interested in us.

But the Lord laid hold on you because He loved you. One of the strangest statements in the word of God is found in John 6:

"All that the Father has given me shall come unto Me; and he that cometh unto Me I will in no wise cast out." We are face to face with something our finite little minds cannot grasp. It is the love of God. "Love is a many splendored thing," as the old song goes. When God loves a person, you cannot explain it—not His love. Oh, you say, "He loves so and so because they are so pure." Well, I was not, and I doubt whether you were.

Why does He love us? "Well," you say, "He loves us because … well … " Well, why does He love you? Oh, do you have special qualities that have caught the eye of the Lord? Is that why He loves you? You cannot explain love.

Why did the Lord lay hold on you? It is because He loved you. He set His love on you. There is no other explanation. But out of that comes something else. It is a fearful thing to be loved by the Lord because He will never let you go. He will arrange your circumstances, your problems, your situations, until every prop that you rest on is destroyed, until in the end your whole life is in Him. That is love.

For what did the Lord lay hold on you? When the Lord laid hold on you, He had a purpose, an eternal purpose. When He laid hold on you, He had in His heart and in His mind something for you, and the apostle says that it is the goal, the prize of the high calling of God in Christ Jesus.

Called to His Eternal Glory

I have three things that I want to underline. The first thing is this. The Lord laid hold on you with glory in mind. Glory! If you know yourself, you are inglorious. I am. There is nothing glorious about me. I am one big mess, a whole bunch of contradictions. Have you discovered that about yourself yet? Have you ever discovered that the word of God says, "We have all sinned and fallen short of the glory of God"?

In 1 Peter 5:10 it says, "The God of all grace who has called you to His eternal glory in Christ Jesus." We are called to His eternal glory. When God took hold of a sinner like you and a sinner like me, a hopeless sinner like you and a hopeless sinner like me, He had glory in mind. There is nothing very glorious about us. Our condition is inglorious. The material that makes us up is inglorious. The very genetic history we have is inglorious. What is there about us that is glorious? We have an unbelievable capacity to sin, an unbelievable capacity for depravity.

"Oh," you might say, "that is no description of me." Let the Lord expose you to the right temptation, the right kind of circumstances, and our depravity becomes a fact. It is the mercy of God that He has not. There is nothing glorious about you and there is nothing glorious about me. But the Lord saved us. He took our Lord Jesus and made Him to be sin for us that we might become God's righteousness in Him. He bore our sin away, and on the basis of what He did at Calvary, God pronounced us righteous in His sight. It is unbelievable! We are righteous in His sight. To use the Biblical word, we are justified in His sight. There is nothing glorious about you, nothing glorious about me, but when He saved you and when He saved me, He had glory in mind.

The more you go on with the Lord, the less you feel that there is glory in you. Yet, the word of God is quite clear. In Colossians 1:27 it says, "This mystery is simple; Christ in you, the hope of glory."

It is not Christ in you, the possible hope of glory, the kind of hope against hope that we shall one day have glory. But it is Christ in you, the certain hope of glory.

Is Christ in you? Are you saved by the grace of God? Are you abiding in the Lord Jesus where God has placed you and therefore He is in you? Then Christ in you is the certain hope of glory. The more there is of the Lord Jesus in you, the more glory there will be. The less of the Lord Jesus in you the less glory there will be. Is there any wonder that the apostle John said, "I must decrease, He must increase?"

With Unveiled Face

In II Corinthians 3:18 we read this wonderful word: "But we all, with unveiled face beholding as in a mirror the glory of the Lord, are transformed into the same image from glory to glory, even as from the Lord the Spirit."

It is the Holy Spirit's work to, as it were, destroy the veil on our face, so that with an unveiled face we can behold as in a mirror the glory of the Lord. As we behold the glory of the Lord, we are changed into His likeness from glory to glory.

When you are in this process, it does not seem like glory to glory. It seems like tribulation to tribulation, affliction to affliction, problem to problem, and from difficulty to difficulty. But that is the way the Lord does it. We are so lazy. I suppose I ought to speak for myself and not for you good Americans. But we are so lazy. Who wants the Lord to enlarge capacity in us for glory when it means tribulation and affliction? Who wants the Lord to do a work in us which is painful?

I know that the one creature in the whole world I fear more than surgeons, doctors, or lawyers is a dentist. I find dentists frightening. "A bit more," they say, "just a bit more." Then they stick all those things in your mouth and tell you jokes. So you nearly swallow the whole lot, if you have a sense of humor. Then they have another look. "Just a little bit more," they say. Pain and pain. I have never responded to anesthetic, so I feel it all the time.

Who is ready for the Lord to increase their capacity for glory? You have to be a kind of spiritual masochist to want the Lord to do this painful job. But we are so lazy. We so love a comfortable, affluent type of Christianity, somehow being carried through it all on a bed of roses. But there is no way to come to the goal, to the prize of the high calling of God in Christ Jesus without glory. And glory means, generally speaking, a lot of problems and a lot of difficulties in our lives. It is the only way. Wouldn't it be wonderful if we could have some spiritual experience that blows us along like some supersonic jet into glory? Poof! And we are there. There is no pain, no problem; we are there. There is no such thing.

I believe that you should have as much experience of the Lord as is possible to contain within your human form. But it does not matter how many experiences you have of the Lord, the creating of a greater capacity for glory, the decrease of your self-life and the increase of the Lord Jesus in you is always with pain and with problems.

Light Affliction

That is why it says in Romans 8:17: "And if children, then heirs; heirs of God, and joint-heirs with Christ; if so be that we suffer with him, that we may be also glorified with him." What a calling! "Heirs of God, joint-heirs with the Lord Jesus." What a calling to share His glory, to share His destiny. Is there any greater calling that a child of God could have?

"If so be that we suffer with Him, that we may be also glorified with Him." There is an "if" here. If you escape the suffering, you will escape the glory because it is the way the Lord uses to increase the capacity for glory.

I think of the Scripture in II Corinthians 4:17–18: "For our light affliction, which is for the moment, worketh for us more and more exceedingly an eternal weight of glory; while we look not at the things which are seen, but at the things which are not seen: for the things which are seen are temporal; but the things which are not seen are eternal."

Did you hear that? The apostle says, "Our light affliction." He can speak of me in this way, but when I think of the apostle's own history, I can hardly call it light affliction. He was stoned, left for dead, rejected by his own people, hounded from synagogue to synagogue. Everywhere his name was an off scouring, his reputation was destroyed, and finally he was in chains writing the greatest letters that have ever been written. He was given revelations from the throne of God while chained to a soldier. He calls it light affliction. He does not say, "Your light affliction." He says, "Our light affliction."

Oh, this man! Do not speak to me about his weaknesses and failings. There is no doubt he had them. That is why the churches in Asia turned away from him. I have always found in my history among the people of God that whenever there is a big hullabaloo, there are nearly always problems in God's servants. If you want to look for problems in them, you will find them. Go on a witch-hunt and you will find them. Do not speak to me about this man's weaknesses and failures. He had an experience of affliction that I would not call light.

Why then does he call it light? It is a question of the glory. If you compare it with the glory, it is light affliction. If we could have him here and question him he would say, "I can explain it very simply. This affliction works glory, and it is light affliction when you compare it with the eternal weight of glory that it produces." It is so simple. It is not easy to see it that way because we look at the things which are seen. If we look at the things which are not seen, it suddenly becomes clear. Yes; and it works for us more and more exceedingly an eternal weight of glory.

Why did the Lord Jesus lay hold of you? It is for glory. He intends that you be glorified, that you share in something of the glory He had when He was transfigured in glory. It was not a spotlight coming on Him from heaven but something happened within Him. A light was turned on and every part of His being radiated light. Glory!

Materials for Glory

I think of that city of God, the bride, the wife of the Lamb. She is produced out of only three materials—gold, precious stone, and pearl. These are the materials for glory. Wood, hay, and stubble are not materials for glory. They can be very beautiful, especially when you have polished teak or rose wood or satin wood. It is so beautiful.

Many, many times I have been taken by friends in Manila to Imelda Marcos' coconut palace. It sounds like a fair ground. It is far from it; it is so beautiful. The floors are coconut, the temples are coconut, all the cushions are made out of coconut. The shades are out of coconut. Everything is out of coconut. Can you believe it! It was the VIP guesthouse of the Filipino Government, and it was Imelda Marcos' great idea.

It was astounding! I went all the way round with a guide saying, "This cannot be coconut."

"Oh, it is, sir."

"What part of coconut is it?"

"It is such and such. The flowers and the leaves are from the outside."

I could not believe it. "Are you really telling us this?"

"No, no," he said, "there is not a single thing in here other than the screws that are anything but coconut." It is so beautiful. They put only the big wigs there. All the VIPs were in this place next to the sea on Manila Bay.

Many Christians are building coconut palaces. They are so beautiful. It looks like a miracle. Oh, how wonderful that Christian life is! What service that is! What kind of church that is! Marvelous! But it is coconut. It will not go through the fire. It is wood, hay, and stubble.

Is your life wood, hay, and stubble? There is no glory in wood, hay, and stubble. Gold is the material for glory, so refined that it is transparent as crystal. Precious stone is mined in the dark places of the earth and then cut, polished, and fitted. That is material for glory.

Pearl is a worthless bit of grit. Grit is the thing that chickens eat to give them good shells for the eggs. If I would say, "Who would like this grit?" there would not be a taker. Who would want a bit of grit? You would say, "Grit! I don't want any grit. There is enough of it out there. It is worthless, trash, rubbish." But at the heart of every real pearl there is a bit of grit. Into the softest part of the clam falls that little bit of worthless rubbish.

It is no wonder that when this happens in your life you say, "This is not the Lord. This cannot be the Lord." It is like the apostle Paul: "Lord, it will destroy my ministry. Take it away from me." But the Lord said, "My grace is sufficient for you." And the coat went round the grit, and another coat, and another coat, and another coat, until lo and behold, you cannot see the grit anymore. You can only see a pearl. Pearls are material for glory.

For what has the Lord laid hold on you and for what has He laid hold on me? It is for glory, that we may be glorified.

Changed into His Likeness

This is the second thing I want to talk about. For what has the Lord laid hold on you? He has laid hold on you that you might be changed into His likeness. In Romans 8:29 it says, "For whom he foreknew, he also foreordained [predestined] to be conformed to the image of his Son, that he might be the first born among many brethren."

When the Lord laid hold of you, it was that you may be changed into His likeness. It is the same kind of word you have in II Corinthians 3:18: "Beholding as in a mirror the glory of the Lord, are transformed into the same image from glory to glory."

So the Lord laid hold of you to change you into His likeness. What a difficult, complex, impossible job! I will say it again: the Lord laid hold of you to change you, transform you into His image, change you into His likeness. What a difficult, complex, impossible job!

You may say, "Oh, I don't know. I do not think He has too far to go with me. I think I am quite like the Lord really." It is an interesting fact that everyone who ever saw the Lord fell at His feet as dead, as if there was something so corruptible that it turned to worms, death ridden, corruption ridden. Every time anyone ever saw the Lord, they felt unclean; they felt corruptible; they felt only mortal. They felt somehow or other that the Lord was a thousand, thousand miles away, so different.

When the apostle Paul wrote one of his early letters, he described himself as the least of all saints. But when he wrote his last letter, he described himself as the chief of all sinners. The nearer he got to the goal, the more unlike the Lord Jesus he felt himself to be.

In this same Philippian letter it says, "Being confident of this very thing, that he who began a good work in you will perfect it until the day of Jesus, the Messiah" (Philippian 1:6).

The Lord is determined to work this in you and in me. Isn't it marvelous! I do not know if you believe in predestination. When I was first saved, I did not. I went right the other way. I believed so much in the free will of man and his responsibility. I remember that godly old missionary in Egypt, Noel Hunt, a New Zealander who used to say to me: "Why do you emphasize so much this matter of free will?" I said, "Because I believe in it." I was an arrogant youngster, eighteen years of age talking to the superintendent of the Egypt General Mission. He must have wondered what he had on his hands. But I had been secunded by the China Inland Mission to the Egypt General Mission to be trained. And I remember how he said to me: "I think there is another side to this coin." It was he who wrote in my autograph book on the day I left Egypt to go back to England: "All that the Father hath given to me shall come unto me, and he that cometh unto me I will in no wise cast him out, and I will raise him on the last day."

I remember reading it and thinking nothing of it. But all these years later I have come to see that it is absolute truth. I do not understand it; I only know that behind our calling is election. But even if you do not agree with me, you will agree with me on this. We are predestined to be conformed to the image of God's Son. This transformation into the image of the Lord Jesus, this being changed into His likeness has behind it all the sovereign power and authority of God. He will not rest until this work is done.

The "I" Problem

Transformed! Do you feel you need to be transformed? This marvelous work begins in our spirit, it is a question of winning our soul, and ends in the redemption of the body. God begins by raising your spirit, which was dead in trespasses and sin, and making it alive to God. So for the first time spiritual eyes are open, spiritual ears are open. You are alive; you are alive to God. That is where it all begins. But then you have the problem of personality, soul. Do not despise your soul. God loves your soul, but your soul is the problem. This is your thought, your emotion, your will—I. Really, it is I. It is your soul life. The bigger the soul, the more pain we feel when the Lord deals with us.

I remember an old Danish missionary telling me what brother Nee said when he saw her colleague, a lady called Amma. She was a church army officer, and boy was she an officer! I knew them both, so I knew what he meant. When brother Nee saw her in 1937 in Denmark, he turned to the Danish missionary and said, "Who is that sister?" And she said, "That is my colleague." "Oh," he said, "what a big soul, and what she will suffer before the Lord wins that soul!"

The more gifted you are and the stronger your soul, the more you will feel the work of the Lord as He changes you. But this is a marvelous thing, this salvation of ours. It is so tremendous, beginning in our spirit, moving into our soul, and ending with a redeemed body, a body glorious like His.

How are we changed? It is not by looking at your self. Many Christians get this idea: "Oh, I must start to investigate myself. Am I really like the Lord Jesus?" Well, you thought you were to begin with. At least there were some traces, but now as you begin to look in, you become more and more depressed. But that is not the way the Lord does it. The way the Lord deals with you and with me is when we behold the glory of the Lord with an unveiled face, as in a mirror. That is when we are changed. That is the healthy way because when you see the Lord, you see your self. Then, when you have your eyes on the Lord, you know that nothing is impossible, not even your being changed into His likeness. So this is a tremendous thing, this whole matter of being transformed into the likeness of the Lord Jesus.

Reigning with Christ

This is the third thing. For what did the Lord lay hold on you and on me? He laid hold on you and He laid hold on me that we might reign with Him. He has a government in mind. He has a throne in mind. He could reign alone, but He does not want to. In the same way that He is bringing many sons to glory, so He will not reign alone. He wants those who will reign with Him.

"To him that overcomes will I grant to sit down with Me in My throne." It is interesting that our Lord Jesus said this to a church where the Head of the church and the Savior of the body was outside. He was plaintively knocking on the door and saying, "If any man hear My voice, let him open the door and I will come in and will sup with him and he with Me." This church was so affluent, so comfortable. It felt that it had such good teaching; it had the whole routine of a good church, the Lord's Table, the prayer meeting, the Bible study, the gospel meeting, and I don't know what else. They thought, "Praise the Lord for this assembly." And the Lord said, "You do not know you are the wretched one and naked and poor and blind. I advise you to buy of Me gold refined in the fire, that you may become rich."

It was to this church that the Lord said, "To him that overcomes will I grant to sit down with Me in My throne." So there is always hope in the most hopeless circumstances and the most hopeless conditions. There is actually real hope because the Lord says, "To this church I am the Amen." In other words, "If anyone will hear Me I can be the Amen to the whole purpose of God for you."

"Reigning with Christ." When the Lord laid hold of you, He had the throne in mind. "Oh," you say, "I do not feel I will be any good for the throne." You have probably got this idea of the throne as was seen in Britain just recently where the celebration was all about wonderful robes, a great crown, golden carriage and everyone sort of bowing and scraping. "Well," you say, "I wouldn't mind that. I think it would be rather nice, everyone waiting on us, everyone acclaiming us, everyone smoothing the way for us. It is rather good."

Education and Discipline for the Throne

But kingship is a question of service. A bad king, a bad queen thinks only of his or her own comfort, but a good king is there for the people. The amazing thing is that if you are a child of God you are destined for the throne of God, but you cannot come to the throne of God without training. A crowned prince has very especial training. He has especial education. Not even the world princes, his brothers have the same education and the same training as he does. He does not have the same discipline either. He has especial discipline.

Whoever is going to reign from the throne, from the moment they are born they are marked out with especial training, especial education, especial discipline. If you are destined for the throne, then the Lord has given the order already: especial training for you, especial education for you, especial discipline for you.

How does this happen? Can you imagine just putting any Tom, Dick, or Harry on the throne? You may say, "Oh, don't bother about education or discipline." But a person who comes to the throne cannot be a baby. You cannot put a baby on the throne. Whenever there was someone below age, they had to have a regent who watched over everything because a baby could not administer anything, could not rule, could not reign as such.

The kingdom of God is filled with spiritual babies. What is the Lord to do? They cannot reign. They have no idea. They cannot even distinguish or discern what the will of God is. This is special training, this is special education, this is special discipline. You might not like it but you will thank God for it later.

The discipline may be hard and you may wonder: "Why, why should I be subjected to these circumstances, to these problems, to these difficulties? Why should I of all people have these difficult relationships?" It is all a question of discipline.

In this matter of education, so often we never see anything until we are in a problem. Then, when we are in a problem, suddenly something dawns on us and we know.

I remember the first time the Lord showed me what the church is. I read a little booklet by Austin Sparks and it said, "The church is Christ." And I thought, now I know what is wrong with this man. Everybody had spoken against him and I had been trying to find out what was wrong. Now I knew as I put the booklet in my pocket. Any Christian knows that the church is not Christ. Christ is the Head; the church is the body of which Christ is the Head. Obviously that is where all the problems were coming from.

But the Lord has enormous humor, and the next day my reading in the Scripture was I Corinthians 12:12: "As the body has many members, yet is one body; so also is Christ." I read it and I thought there must be a mistake here. It must mean: "As the body has many members and all the members being many are one body, so also is the church of which Christ is head."

I looked it up and I found it says, "So also is Christ." Suddenly, in a flash the Lord said to me: "Don't you see? All your hands, your feet, every part of you are Lance Lambert. Don't you see?" That was the moment, without any pain, my being a fanatical Baptist died a natural death. At that moment I became a Christian. I belonged to every other believer and every other believer belonged to me. What an amazing thing it is!

I remember a wonderful sister who is with the Lord now for quite a number of years, but in earlier years, she meant much to me. She came from a very aristocratic family, a very wealthy lady, and she got mentally ill. In those days, you never mentioned the word "mental illness." Of course, I don't know what they call it here in the States but I think they changed it to "mentally challenged."

She was unwell and the doctor said to her, "You have to go into a hospital."

"What kind of hospital?" she said.

"A special hospital," he said.

She said to me years later that as she was being taken into the hospital she thought: "I feel like I am going into hell. What will my family think when they know that I am in such a place and I am a Christian? What will they think about a person who is a Christian being mentally ill?"

As she went through the doors on a stretcher, she said in her heart, "I am in hell." And the Lord said to her: "Even in hell Thou art there." That is in Psalm 139: "If I dwell in the depths of the sea or the heights of the heaven, but even in hell, Thou, the Lord art there." In that moment she was healed.

When the doctor came to her after making all the tests, he said, "What is wrong with you? There has been a misdiagnosis. There is nothing wrong with you."

"No," she said, "there isn't." And she walked out.

This is education. It is only when you come to a place where you are in a colossal problem, you are at your wit's end, then suddenly the word becomes real. Then God's word becomes yours in a way that will never be taken away. That Scripture becomes yours. That word of the Lord is applied to you by the Holy Spirit. It becomes yours in a way that is nobody else's. It means something to you that it cannot mean to anybody else.

Training for the Throne

Then there is training. Do you realize why the Lord may have given you a very difficult boss? "Oh," you say, "I am going to change jobs." No, do not do that. Maybe it is better for you to have that boss. Or maybe you have some difficult employees or difficult co-workers. It is a much easier thing to get away from them. Do not get away from them. It is part of God's training. You do not realize it but you are under the situation and you cannot get above. Now you are being trained to rule in a situation which is very unpleasant.

Mr. Sparks once told me an amazing story when he was a young man in his teens. He got saved, wonderfully saved. Dr. F. B. Meyer meant a lot to him and he went to talk to him. When he arrived at his appointment, Dr. Meyer's wife showed him into his study and said he would be there in a few minutes. Brother Sparks sat in the study, and like all young men, he began to look around at the books that the great man had. Suddenly, on the mantel piece he saw a wooden plaque with letters in gold. It just said two words: "Look down." And he said, "I was transfixed. What does that mean? Surely it is, 'Look up.'"

At that moment Dr. F. B. Meyer came in and noticed that Austin Sparks' eyes were riveted on that little piece of wood. He said, "Oh, you have seen that little motto on the mantel piece."

"Yes," said Mr. Sparks, "but shouldn't it be, 'Look up'?"

Dr. F. B. Meyer said, "It is a question of your position. If you are under something, look up, but when you are seated with Christ in heavenly places, look down."

In other words, when you learn how to reign with Christ over practical situations in your home, in your business, at school, at work, in the church, in the work of the Lord, when you learn practically, in reality, what it is to sit with Christ, you look down. You see every situation from the throne. Do you understand? We are being trained.

When the Lord is speaking to you and me and saying that He is bringing many sons to glory, it is sons. He is not bringing many babes to glory; He is bringing many sons to glory. A son can reign; a babe cannot. A babe, a child is a matter of relationship to the Lord, to the Father, but a son has not only that relationship, he is able to take over the family business. This is so tremendous that you and I have been laid hold on by the Lord Jesus to bring us to reign with him. It requires training. It requires education. It requires discipline.

To Endure

One of the most beautiful words is overcoming. "To him that overcomes." We have given it such a kind of meaning that we are almost frightened of it. But all it means is "to endure." To endure and still be in the center of the will of God in spite of everything—that is overcoming. To be in the work of the Lord where the Lord wants you—that is overcoming. To be in the midst of the church when there are messes, factions, divisions, much that is negative, and still serve the Lord, and still wash the feet of your brothers and sisters—that is overcoming.

"To him that overcomes, to him that wins through, to him that comes out on top, will I grant to sit down with Me in My throne, even as also I overcame and sat down with My Father in His throne." The Lord has laid hold on you with a goal, a tremendous goal in view. You need to press on. Do not let the things which are behind chain you or destroy you or cause you to cast away your confidence. You have a goal, and when the Lord laid His hand on you, when He took hold of you, it was that goal He had in view.

May the Lord help each one of us by the grace of God and by the power of God to reach that goal and obtain that prize.

Shall we pray:

Beloved Lord, we want to thank You from our heart that You are the One who has laid hold of us. We rather thought we had come to You but in the first case, You took hold of us. And Lord, we want to pray that You will open our eyes to see what it is that You have laid hold on us for. Open our eyes, Lord. Some of us may be in danger of casting away our confidence because we feel we are in such a mess and our circumstances are so difficult and our problems so many and the obstacles so great. But Lord, we pray that You will help us to submit to You in the right way; not to take on anything that we should not take on, but that we might learn of You. Beloved Lord, hear us in this prayer. We see the goal before us, Lord. Will You by Your grace open our eyes in a new understanding of what it is that You have laid hold of us for. We ask it in the name of our Lord Jesus. Amen.

3.
The Bride and God's Home

Philippians 3:7–14

Howbeit what things were gain to me, these have I counted loss for Christ. Yea verily, and I count all things to be loss for the excellency of the knowledge of Christ Jesus my Lord: for whom I suffered the loss of all things, and do count them but refuse, that I may [win] gain Christ, and be found in him, not having a righteousness of mine own, even that which is of the law, but that which is through faith in Christ, the righteousness which is from God by faith:

that I may know him, and the power of his resurrection, and the fellowship of his sufferings, becoming conformed unto his death; if by any means I may attain unto the resurrection from the dead. Not that I have already obtained, or am already made perfect: but I press on, if so be that I may lay hold on that for which also I was laid hold on by Christ Jesus. Brethren, I count not myself yet to have laid hold: but one thing I do, forgetting the things which are behind, and stretching

forward to the things which are before, I press on toward the goal unto the prize of the high calling of God in Christ Jesus.

Revelation 21:1–5a

And I saw a new heaven and a new earth: for the first heaven and the first earth are passed away; and the sea is no more. And I saw the holy city, new Jerusalem, coming down out of heaven from God, made ready as a bride adorned for her husband. And I heard a great voice out of the throne saying, Behold, the tabernacle of God is with men, and he shall dwell with them, and they shall be his peoples, and God himself shall be with them, and be their God: and he shall wipe away every tear from their eyes; and death shall be no more; neither shall there be mourning, nor crying,

nor pain, any more: the first things are passed away. And he that sitteth on the throne said, Behold, I make all things new

Revelation 21:22

And I saw no temple therein: for the Lord God the Almighty, and the Lamb, are the temple thereof.

Ephesians 2:19–22

So then ye are no more strangers and sojourners, but ye are fellow-citizens with the saints, and of the household of God, being built upon the foundation of the apostles and prophets, Christ Jesus himself being the chief corner stone; in whom [the whole building] each several building, fitly framed together, groweth into a holy temple in the Lord; in whom ye also are builded together for a habitation of God in the Spirit.

Shall we pray:

Beloved Lord, we are so thankful that You have provided us with an anointing. In that anointing there is an open heaven. And we praise You, beloved Lord, that You do not leave us to our own energies or talents or gifts, but You have provided us with that anointing of grace and power both for the speaking of Your word and the hearing of Your word. We dare not approach the ministry of Your word without recognizing that we are totally dependent upon You. By faith, we stand into that anointing which has been so dearly won by our Lord Jesus at Calvary and made such a reality in the gift of the Holy Spirit. Beloved Lord, let that anointing come upon us all, and grant that Your purpose in our time be fulfilled. We shall be careful, Lord, to give You all the thanks and praise of our hearts for answering our prayer. We ask it in the name of our Lord Jesus. Amen

We have been considering this remarkable testimony of the apostle Paul contained in this third chapter of the Philippian letter. Of all the many testimonies in the Bible this, in my estimation, is the most remarkable of them all. Apart from anything else it raises some very serious questions and I have sought to raise those questions. This is not in order to confuse you but in order that we might understand what the apostle is seeking by the Spirit of God to say to us.

I spoke of three things for which I believe the Lord laid hold on you and me. The first was glory, the second was to change us into His likeness, and the third was to bring us to reign with Him in His throne. Here you have three tremendous matters. Why did He lay hold of you? He laid hold of you that you in the end might share His glory. You might be glorified. Why did He lay hold of you? That He might change you into His likeness. Why did He lay hold of you? That He might bring you to His throne to reign with Him. That requires, of course, training, education, and discipline.

The Bride

Now I have two more matters. This is the first one. For what did the Lord take hold of you? Why did He lay hold on you? It is because He loved you. But for what did the Lord take hold on you? It is to be His bride. This is not a sentimental word but it is a tremendous matter.

The Bible begins with a wedding and ends with a wedding. It begins with a wedding that is a human marriage until death parted Adam and Eve, and it ends with a marriage between the Lamb and the wife of the Lamb. The amazing thing is that in one sense the whole Bible from Genesis to Revelation is all about this love of God for us and this quest for a bride for His Son. Of course, God is using Sunday School language if I may so say. How else could He speak to us? If He spoke to us in highly scientific language, if He tried to speak about principles, many of us would be totally lost from the very beginning. But God takes the simplest things, things that all of us know about, things that all of us generally experience, and uses them as the means to bring home the truth to us.

Why does the Bible end with a marriage? It is a very good question. You would not think normally that a book like the Bible with sixty-six books would end with a marriage. The marriage supper of the Lamb is first and then a little later we see this amazing marriage. And the last picture we get, if I may put it in my own words, is the Lamb and the wife of the Lamb going out into the ages to come. We do not know what they are going to do. We do not know if God is going to create new universes. We do not know what He is going to do with this old heaven and earth. It will be a new heaven and earth by then. But what is He going to do when everything is released from the corruption, when this wonderful world in which we live (and we are making such a mess of), given on trust to us by God, will one day be restored and know that redemption of God and everything will be reconciled to God through our Lord Jesus? Wonderful!

We have no idea what is stored up for us. The Scripture says that it is beyond imagination, beyond the capacity of our finite little brains to understand, beyond even our little hearts to take in. It is something so tremendous that the Bible speaks of the former things having passed away, and He is making all things new. But we do not really know what this "all things new" entails. We only know that God ends the Bible with a marriage, as if God is saying, "This is the key to eternity; this is the key to the ages to come." The key is very simple: it is a bride for the Lamb. When those two are finally brought together, the bride is prepared, produced, as it were, created, as it were, trained, as it were, she has grown up, as it were. Finally there comes the marriage, and that is the end of the Bible.

We have so many questions. Will we wear clothes in eternity? It always seems to interest Germans and Swedes. I do not know why. It does not seem to bother Asians quite so much. Will we eat in the ages to come? The Chinese are always asking me this. Will we recognize one another in the ages to come? What will we do? How will we do it? Will God do it apart from us? Or will He use us to do it? There are thousands of questions that we have. We cannot answer these questions. Some people have gotten themselves into what I call speculative theology, which is taking one little phrase and developing a whole idea and concept of what might happen in the ages to come. Let us stay with what is revealed to us.

What is it that God reveals to us? He is seeking for a bride and once that bride and the Lamb are joined together in an eternal union, the wedding takes place. Then the Lord can get on with the job. In many ways that is a very salutary lesson for us to learn. If we are going to be caught on a thousand and one questions as to what we will do, what we will eat, whether we will recognize each other, who will be there and who will not be there, will we be able to see hell (another question some people ask me who seem to be very upset at the thought that they are going to be in glory and see the smoke as it were coming up from hell), that is not the point. Don't escape the real point. The real point is that when you were saved by the grace of God, the Lord Jesus took hold of you to be His bride. It is as simple as that. He took hold of you that He might bring you as a bride to Himself.

Wherever you look in the Bible you will find it. If you open your Bible roughly in the center, you have a little book called The Song of Songs. Liberal theologians call it a bawdy ditty. That is how more than one has described it. But in the Jewish tradition it is an allegory of the love between God and His redeemed given in a vision to King Solomon. There you have the most amazing picture, we could say in New Testament terms, of the Lamb and His bride, so intimate, so full of tenderness, so full of grace, so full of love, and so full of beauty. It is an amazing story right at the heart of the Bible.

When John the apostle wrote his gospel, it was not like the other three gospels, Matthew, Mark, and Luke, which were histories. His gospel was an interpretation. He chose eight signs and eight declarations of the Lord Jesus: "I AM." He says that the Messianic ministry of the Lord Jesus began with a wedding at Cana of Galilee, as if John was saying, "You see what it is all about? It is a wedding, not something that is corruptible but something incorruptible. He turned water into wine."

John the Baptist, describing himself in the third chapter of John, says, "I am the best man." That is how he described his ministry, his function, his calling. He said, "I am the best man," of the Bridegroom. "I am not the Bridegroom; I am only the best man. But I rejoice to hear the voice of the Bridegroom."

All of this is quite amazing. It ought to wake us up to something. When the Lord laid hold of me, when the Lord laid hold of you, it was to bring us to be His bride, to prepare us to be His bride, to fashion us as His bride.

A Bride Symbolizes Love

What does it symbolize? I think a bride symbolizes love. When our Lord Jesus was asked what is the greatest commandment in the Bible, He answered in Mark's Gospel 12:28: "Hear, O Israel the Lord thy God, the Lord is one. Thou shall love the Lord thy God with all thy heart, with all thy soul, and with all thy strength; and thou shall love thy neighbor as thy self. Upon these two hang the whole law and the prophets."

In other words, the Lord Jesus said, "The whole Bible is summed up in two commandments: 'You shall love the Lord your God with all your heart (heart speaks of spirit), all your soul (that is your personality), and all your strength. And you shall love your neighbor as yourself.'"

Some Christians stuff their heads with Biblical knowledge, and it is a good thing to study the word. It is an even better thing to memorize the word. I thank God that I was taught to memorize the word of God. But we can miss the whole point of the word of God. We can study it, we can get our doctrine sound and correct, and altogether fail on this one great point that God looks for: "Thou shall love the Lord thy God with all thy heart and with all thy soul and with all thy strength." And if you love the Lord your God in such a way, then you will also love your neighbor as yourself.

The prophet Jeremiah was called to one of the most difficult ministries in the whole of the old covenant. And when he was so fed up with the people of God, so sick of their backsliding, so sick of the way they had prostituted themselves to other gods, the Lord appeared to him and said, "I have loved you with an everlasting love; therefore with steadfast love, with persevering love, with merciful, covenant love, I will draw you. Again shall you be built up, oh virgin of Israel." I find that one of the most extraordinary declarations of God in the word of God.

When you have lost your virginity, you can never restore it. It is gone forever. Israel was a prostitute, an adulteress. She had given herself to every kind of pagan, demon god and principality. Yet the Lord said, "I have loved you with an everlasting love. Therefore with this merciful love, this covenant love, this persevering love, this enduring love, I will draw you. Again shall you be built, o virgin of Israel." Interestingly, he speaks of the vineyards of Samaria and of Judea, and you cannot really spiritualize that. So it is clear that it is a message to Israel. It is also an amazing revelation of the love of God for those He redeemed. He will not give them up. He will not forsake them. He will not allow even their wickedness and sin, though it will bring them into judgment, finally to divorce Him from them. He loves with an everlasting love.

One of the simplest little phrases in the New Testament is contained in John's first letter: "God is love." It almost seems trite in one way. It is so simple: "God is love." But within those three words is a profoundness that no child of God has ever fully plumbed, and no child of God has ever been able fully to explain. God is love, not at the expense of His righteousness or His holiness or His justice, but He is love. And love looks always for love. Do not talk to me about being a bride, as if it is just something to do with the outward façade of church life. The key to this whole symbolism is that because God loves He looks for love in you. And the severest censure that the Lord ever brings is when that love has been lost. Because of lukewarmness the Lord says of the Laodicean church, "I will vomit you out of My mouth. You are neither cold nor hot. I would rather you were ice cold than tepid."

Oh dear brothers and sisters, how many of us are tepid! Our service is tepid. Everything about our lives is tepid. It is neither hot nor cold. If God is love, He will never be satisfied with you working your fingers to the bone without love. He will never be satisfied with you just merely singing. He will never be satisfied with you merely praying. He will never even be satisfied with your sacrifice if there is no love, as if it is duty, as if you feel bound to do it. The one thing He looks for is that flame of love. That is why our Lord Jesus, the risen, glorified ascended Messiah speaking to the churches, says to the church at Ephesus: "I have this against you. You have left your first love."

First love is a quality of love. It is not a question of the timing of love. Oh, at the very beginning we had puppy love and that is first love. Then after that we have more of an academic love, a sort of phlegmatic love. It is not what the Lord means by first love. When He speaks about first love, He is speaking about a quality of love. When you fall in love with somebody, nothing is too much.

You dear ladies, surely when you have fallen in love, you are prepared to go to football games when they do not even interest you. You will do anything just because you have fallen in love. You will go anywhere.

You fellows will do anything when you first truly have fallen in love. You will journey not just a few miles; you will journey hundreds of miles just to see the person you love. It is nothing to you. If someone says to you, "Good gracious, did you drive two hundred miles?" "Yes." It does not mean anything. What does it mean to somebody in love? But when you have fallen out of love, when the first love is gone, just to walk down the driveway is too much. Just to do a few small things is too much. But when you are in love and you know your love loves apricot roses, you will give her apricot roses even though they cost fifty dollars a piece. You will do anything. It is first love.

That is the kind of love God looks for in His bride. He wants the kind of love that is a quality of love. It never moans about how much it is suffering. It never moans about the tribulations and the afflictions. It does not moan all the time about the cost of this whole thing. It costs me so much. First love is a quality of love. That is the love the Lord looks for in this bride. Nothing else satisfies the Lord.

In that very well known passage in 1 Corinthians 13:1–2 it says, "If I speak with the tongues of men and of angels, but have not love, I am become sounding brass, or a clanging cymbal. And if I have the gift of prophecy, and know all mysteries and all knowledge (not just a little); and if I have all faith, so as to remove mountains, but have not love, I am nothing."

All mysteries, all knowledge, all faith, but no love equals nothing. Doesn't that find you out? Doesn't that find me out? For what did the Lord lay hold on you? It is to be His bride. But the one thing He is looking for is that love of your heart. Have you left your first love? Have you lost your first love? Has it grown cold? Or is it tepid, lukewarm? Isn't it interesting that in this same passage in chapter 14:1, Phillips translated this years ago: "Make love your aim."

You remember what the Lord Jesus said to Peter after the whole of his self-manufactured Christianity had been blown away in an almighty explosion, when he denied his Lord three times with oaths? "Do you love Me more than these others?" He said it three times. Peter could only come up to: "I have an affection for You." He could not bring upon his lips the words: "I love You" because he knew he had failed. So many times he had made claims which he had never kept, as it were, never lived.

The Lord does not want people sitting around doe-eyed, all kind of mystical, looking up. There is a kind of Christian like this. They are born that way. They were like that before they were saved. They are kind of doe-eyed and starry-eyed. They cannot quite walk straight anyway. The Lord said, "Feed My lambs. Tend My sheep. Feed My sheep."

This love of God, this love in us produced by the Holy Spirit is to be the basis and energy of all service. Peter was the one to whom the Lord Jesus said, "You are a little piece of the rock. Upon this great massive of the rock I will build My church, and the gates of Hell shall not prevail against it. To you have I given the keys to the kingdom of heaven"; not meaning to a papacy, not meaning to a Vatican, but to the whole church of God. It is the love of God that lies at the basis. It has to be the energy for this whole thing.

We hear quite a bit about the bride. We hear so much about the bride preparing herself for the coming of the Lord, all of which is absolutely essential. But if there is no love it means nothing. It is teaching. It is a doctrine. It is a theory. It is something that some gather around as a kind of special teaching. If we believe that He laid hold of us to bring us to be His bride, the one thing we have to guard is that flame of love in our hearts.

"O Thou who camest from above, the pure celestial fire to impart; kindle a sacred flame of love on the mean altar of my heart. There let it burn with inextinguishable blaze, and trembling to its source return in humble prayer and fervent praise."

A Bride Represents Union and Communion

In the whole word of God the bride speaks of this love. But I would like to take it one step further. She represents union and communion. Communion can only come out of union. Union is you and the Lord becoming one. "He that is joined to the Lord is one spirit." "Your life is hid with Christ in God." "When Christ who is our life shall appear, then shall we also appear with Him in glory." "Christ who is our life"—that is union. That is what the Lord is looking for. He is looking for a bride absolutely one with Him, that is identified with Him, identified with His nature, identified with His destiny, identified with His character, identified with His work. Such is the kind of bride that the Lord looks for.

The apostle said in this Philippian letter, "For me to live is Christ." That is union. Out of that comes everything.

In Romans 6:4 it speaks of being buried with Him in baptism that we might be raised with Him to walk in newness of life. You cannot walk in newness of life without that union with the Lord Jesus.

Communion comes out of union. I know these are old-fashioned words, theological words really—union and communion. But how else can we say them? Oneness—maybe that is a more modern way of putting it. I do not know if we can find another word for communion because the whole idea is communion. And it is something to do with union.

What is communion? Communion is intimacy and it comes out of oneness, continuous intimacy. Communion is sensitivity. You are sensitive. That is the kind of bride the Lord is looking for. In Psalm 25:14 it says, "The secret of the Lord is with them that fear him, and he will show them His covenant."

Many people can study all about the covenant theologically, but oh, to really see the covenant with the eyes of the heart! Some versions say "friendship" but the Hebrew word is "sod" which means secret. "The secret of the Lord is with them that fear him." That is not the fear that has torment in it. It is the fear of love, sensitive love. It is a kind of reverential fear of the Lord, a kind of sensitive love for the Lord. It means the Lord will share His secret with you; He will open His heart to you.

Sometimes people come to me and say, "I want the Lord to show me things." I was once like that. I gave those two old missionaries in Port Said such a time. Every time they raised something I would go at them like a dog with a bone. I would not let them go. I kept on and on, and in the end, Miss Liblick, who was Estoninian, (and she looked like a stone) said to me, "There is too much flesh in you." I sort of blinked at her. Then she said, "You have got to have everything laid out all the time before you. You have to know it; you have to see it. This is not the way. You must humble yourself and ask the Lord, 'Are You going to show me this?' And if He does not, put a little mark in your Bible beside it with the date. That is what I do." I come back sometimes a week later, sometimes a month later, and I wonder why I put that there. That is clear to me. I respected her; she was a walking Bible. I had never met anybody like her and Miss Smith. They were two walking Bibles.

If you go on with the Lord, then it becomes clear, but if you come running, running, running about something, you miss what the Lord does want to show you by your worrying about what He is not going to show you. Then you can get all arrogant. That is why it says, "The meek will He teach in his way." Another word for being meek is "teachable."

"The secret of the Lord is with those who fear Him and He will show them His covenant." That means the Lord will unveil it all. He will open it all up to you step by step, stage by stage. Oh, to be sensitive!

I spoke about Lady Ogle, an aristocratic lady, and I thank God for her input in my life in earlier years. She is now with the Lord. I remember a wonderful story she told me. Before she went to Egypt, she had to go before the mission board. She was a very wealthy lady, as well as a titled lady. One of those old gentlemen with a butterfly collar, very, very correct, as only the English can be, looked at her very gravely and said, "Lady Olga, why are you going to the Egyptians?"

"Oh," she said, "I believe the Lord has called me."

Another old gentleman eyed her very severely and said, "Do you love them?"

And she said, "No, I do not." But because she was a very wealthy lady and a titled lady, they still accepted her as a missionary. I think any other candidate would have been put out. But they accepted her on the spot, and out she went to Egypt.

When she got to Egypt (I knew Egypt having lived there), she said, "I had never seen anything more terrible or dirty or unhygienic or depraved than Egypt. The more I saw of it, the more I disliked the Egyptians." Then she began to say, "Why, did You call me, Lord?" She never got an answer from the Lord.

She was attached as a young missionary to a lady missionary doctor. One day while she was there, someone came in and said, "Doctor, come quickly. So and so is lying at the gate of the city. She seems to have had a collapse." Now this lady was a very well known prostitute, and she had syphilis. She was covered with sores. So the doctor told Lady Ogle to go with her. On the way the doctor said, "Now listen, you are going to have to hold her while I give her an injection. It is going to be very unpleasant. She is covered with sores and you can smell her a yard or two away."

When Lady Ogle got there, at first she did not want to go near this person, but the doctor asked her to hold her shoulders. She knelt down and held her and she said to me that the stench was so terrible. And she lifted her heart and said, "Oh God, how do people ever get into a mess like this? I cannot love them." And the Lord said to her, "Kiss her." Lady Ogle thought she would catch a thousand and one things, so she hesitated. The Lord said a second time: "Kiss her." Then Lady Ogle said to me: "I bent over and kissed her on her forehead. Then I kissed her on the cheek and on her lips. And my heart was filled with love for the Egyptians."

Sensitivity. So much about evangelism is like a bull in a china shop. It is like a tank looming over me. There is so little sensitivity. But in the end, it is this sensitivity of love that the Lord looks for. I know I fall very far short in this. I imagine you do too. But when you take that step of faith, you will find that the love of God is shed abroad in your heart. What you could never love naturally, your heart will be filled with love.

The Home of God

The second thing I want to underline is that when the Lord laid hold of you, He laid hold of you to make you with Him the eternal home of God. When you come to the last chapters of the Bible, you read these wonderful words: "And God will tabernacle amongst men and He will dwell with them forever."

It encompasses so much of the Bible. Tabernacle! Tabernacle! Temple! Did you notice that there is no temple therein, but the Lord God, the Almighty, and the Lamb are the temple thereof? Did you know that this holy city, this bride, this wife of the

Lamb is a cube? It is one thousand, two hundred miles this way, one thousand, two hundred miles in breadth, and one thousand, two hundred miles high—a cube. Did you know that the Holy of Holies was a cube? In other words, the place where God dwelt, where there was no light, the glory of God lit it. The Holy of Holies was a cube. What is God saying? God is simply saying, "I have come home. It is home. Finally, I have found My home." Again, we are dealing with Sunday School language.

I feel so sorry for any human being that does not have a home. How many psychological problems are due to homelessness! What is home? Home is the place you can rest. Home is the place where you can be yourself. Home is where you do not have to bother what you look like. You can be absolutely yourself. That is home.

God takes this picture of a home and uses it in Sunday School language to say, "That is what I am looking for. I do not find my home in mountains or in lakes or in the atmosphere or in the seas or on the earth. I find My home in human beings who have been saved by the finished work of My Son. That is My home. And once I have come home I can express Myself. I can be Myself."

You will find this in the Bible in so many places. For instance, you find it in Deuteronomy 33:27: "The eternal God is thy dwelling place, and underneath are the everlasting arms." This is a strange combination— "The eternal God is thy dwelling place and underneath are the everlasting arms."

"The Lord has chosen Zion for his habitation (his home); this is my resting place forever. Here will I dwell" (see Psalm 132:13–14).

It is one thing for the Lord to visit, it is one thing for the Lord to bless, it is one thing for the Lord to use; it is another thing for the Lord to come home. When the Lord comes home, it is to dwell forever.

In the prophecy of Ezekiel, from chapters 40—48, there is an amazing picture of this city, this house of the Lord, the river that comes out of it, and the tree on either side of the river. In Revelation 21 and 22, you see the most amazing connection. But at the end of Ezekiel, it says, "And the name of this city shall be called in Hebrew Adonai-shammah, the Lord is there." He has come home. Finally, He has come home.

A Home of God in Christ

Do you know why the Lord Jesus laid hold of you? He laid hold of you to build you into a temple. He laid hold of you to make you His home. This is what it says in Ephesians 2:20–21: "Being built upon the foundation of the apostles and prophets, Christ Jesus Himself being the chief cornerstone; in whom the whole building, fitly framed together, groweth into a holy temple in the Lord."

In whom? In the Lord Jesus. In Christ the whole building is fitly framed together and is growing into a holy temple in the Lord. In whom? In Christ you also are being built together for a home of God in the Spirit. You cannot get beyond that.

When God comes home, you will come home. In other words, you will be homeless until God comes home. When God comes home, you will no longer be homeless. That is why the Holy Spirit's work now is to build us together, to bring us into a shared life. It is not easy.

The Lord Jesus said in John 2, "Destroy this temple and in three days I will raise it up." Oh, that caused some fuss. The scribes and the chief priests were so upset. They said, "This building has taken all these years to build and He is going to destroy the thing? This is going to lead to rebellion? Is He is going to try to bring sort of a riotous tumult into this place and wreck it?" But Jesus was speaking of His body. It is not just His personal body; it is a corporate body. He is speaking about Himself as the dwelling place of God, the home of God.

The Lord Jesus made an extraordinary statement that is contained in Matthew 16:18: "Upon this rock I will build my church; and the gates of hell shall not prevail against it." There could not be anything simpler or clearer. He said, "My church." It is not a church; "My church." This incredible statement the Lord Jesus made is so significant. Indeed, I would say it is strategically significant because it explains the whole of this age. "Upon this rock I will build my church." It came as a result of Him saying, "Who do men say that I am?" And they said, "Some say Jeremiah, some others say prophets." "Who do you say I am?" Before anyone could say anything, Peter said, "You are the Messiah, the Son of the living God."

And Jesus said, "Flesh and blood did not reveal that to you but My Father who is in heaven." Out of that divine revelation concerning the Person of the Lord Jesus came this clear, dogmatic statement: "Upon this rock I will build My church."

He said, "You are Peter (Petros), and upon this massive of the rock, (Petra) I will build My church." What was the Lord Jesus saying? "Peter, you are a small stone but upon this massive rock I will build My church."

Years later, Peter wrote by the Spirit what he understood of that statement of the Lord Jesus. In 1 Peter 2:4–5 he said, "Unto whom coming a living stone, elect, precious (the Lord Jesus), ye also as living stones are built up a spiritual house, to be a holy priesthood to offer up spiritual sacrifices acceptable to God through Jesus Christ."

Living Stones

The Lord Jesus is a living stone. We also are living stones, all quarried out of the eternal life of God, being built together. It is not enough to have a stone here and a stone there. It is not enough even to have a pile of stones or even have stones sort of put very tidily. That is not a house; that is not a home. They have to find their relationship to one another. So when the Lord laid hold of you with this eternal home of God in mind, it requires you to find relationship to other brothers and sisters, and that is the problem. If we could only make our own way to glory, it would be so much easier Being built together is no pleasant business. There are times when it is wonderful, times when a spirit of worship is present, times when the spirit of revelation is present, times when the spirit of fellowship is present, times when the spirit of love is present. But there are other times when it is one big shindig, and everybody is sort of negative and critical.

If only this church were invisible! If only in some wonderful way you and I, as members of the church, could somehow be built in some mystical way that we hardly know how or where we are built into it.

But when you come to Matthew 18 you find that the Lord is speaking about a problem that a brother has with another brother. He said, "Go to him alone. If he listens to you, you have won him; if he does not listen, take others, two or three witnesses. Then, if he does not listen, go to the church."

"Whatsoever you bind on earth shall be bound in heaven. Again I say to you, 'If two of you shall agree on earth as touching anything that they shall ask you, it shall be done for them of My Father who is in heaven, for where two or three are gathered together in My name, there am I in the midst."

Here is a church on earth in time in place. It is a very imperfect church, a church where brothers fall out, where brothers find themselves incompatible. And it is not just brothers; it is sisters too. Brothers can be very catty when they want to. We don't use the word catty. I suppose we should use the word doggy. Oh, the problems we have in the church!

Everyone is searching for the perfect church. There is no such thing as the perfect church down here. By its very nature, it is imperfect. If we could only get a little elite group together of going-on saints, all overcomers, all devoted to the Lord, all pure in mind, all seeing the Lord, all hearing the Lord, all warring the warfare, wouldn't it be wonderful? But then, if in one of our prayer meetings this perfect little church gets on its knees and says, "Lord, save. We do not just want this church to be ourselves. We want you to save men and women." And God saves three thousand. Our perfect little fellowship is now imperfect, because into our fellowship have come drug addicts, alcoholics, divorcees, people who are gay, and I do not know what else.

They are saved and we say thank God for that. They are born again, cleansed. Yes they are, but those of us who have had anything to do with human beings in the church of God know very well that a drug addict is not delivered just over night. Perhaps he is delivered from the drugs but the thing that led him to it takes time for the Holy Spirit to really work out. It is the same with alcoholism, and the thing that led to divorce, the thing that led to all the other incompatibilities, collisions, and unhappinesses.

In the churches at the beginning of Revelation, there was Nicolaitanism, there was a Jezebel in one of them teaching the deep things of Satan. Have you ever heard of anything like it? I can just hear some people saying, "We are getting out of here." But they were real churches, and they were to stay and overcome. It is when we wash one another's feet that we really overcome. When our Lord took that bowl of water and washed the disciples' feet, you could have said, "What is He doing washing Peter's feet? Peter is going to deny Him this very night and He is washing his feet? Ridiculous!" And Judas! He even stole from the treasury. What was Jesus doing? The Lord Jesus said, "I have left you an example of what you should do to one another."

This home of God, this holy temple of the Lord is Sunday School language. Have you any idea what is in store for us when God comes home? It will be glory; it will be fulness; it will be life; it will be joy. There is no end to what lies ahead of those who are born of God. But are we prepared for such a prize?

For what did the Lord lay hold on you? It is that you might be His eternal home. When the Holy Spirit brought the Lord Jesus to birth, it was as if God found the beginning of His home on earth in a human being. When He was thirty years of age, heaven opened and the Spirit came down upon Him, and John said, "And dwelt upon Him." God had found His home but it was one Person. On the day of Pentecost when the Holy Spirit was poured out by the risen Head of the church, it was as if God found His home in one hundred and twenty members of the body of the Lord Jesus. Within hours it had grown to three thousand, one hundred and twenty. And so it went on and on and on.

What a tremendous thing it is that the Lord laid hold of you and the Lord laid hold of me! But do we know this goal? Do we know this is the goal to which we are pressing? Do we know that there is a prize of this high calling of God in Christ Jesus to be won? May the Lord open our eyes and touch our hearts.

Shall we pray:

Dear Lord, You say to every one of us in this place: "Do you love Me? Do you love Me more than these? Feed My lambs. Tend My sheep. Feed My sheep." Beloved Lord, our prayer is that You will open the eyes of our hearts. Preserve us, Lord, from a mere sound but legal understanding of the bride and Your home. Lord, by Your Spirit bring us to the place where we realize that You love us, that You actually love each one of us, and You are waiting for a response in our hearts. If we have grown tepid, if we have grown lukewarm, have mercy upon us. Don't vomit us out, Lord. Have mercy upon us. By Your Spirit touch us. Lord, wrestle with us. Bring us to a new place altogether. Hear us. We do not want to be the same. We want to be a people filled with Your beauty, filled with Your grace, and filled with Your love. So hear us, Lord. We ask it in the name of our Lord Jesus. Amen.

4.
Laying Hold

Philippians 3:7–14

Howbeit what things were gain to me, these have I counted loss for Christ. Yea verily, and I count all things to be loss for the excellency of the knowledge of Christ Jesus my Lord: for whom I suffered the loss of all things, and do count them but refuse, that I may [win] gain Christ, and be found in him, not having a righteousness of mine own, even that which is of the law, but that which is through faith in Christ, the righteousness which is from God by faith:

that I may know him, and the power of his resurrection, and the fellowship of his sufferings, becoming conformed unto his death; if by any means I may attain unto the resurrection from the dead. Not that I have already obtained, or am already made perfect: but I press on, if so be that I may lay hold on that for which also I was laid hold on by Christ Jesus. Brethren, I count not myself yet to have laid hold: but one thing I do, forgetting the things which are behind, and stretching

forward to the things which are before, I press on toward the goal unto the prize of the high calling of God in Christ Jesus.

Ephesians 1:16–23

[I] cease not to give thanks for you, making mention of you in my prayers; that the God of our Lord Jesus Christ, the Father of glory, may give unto you a spirit of wisdom and revelation in the knowledge of him; having the eyes of your heart enlightened, that ye may know what is the hope of his calling, what the riches of the glory of his inheritance in the saints, and what the exceeding greatness of his power to us-ward who believe, according to that working of the strength of his might which he wrought in Christ, when he raised him from the dead, and made him to sit at his right hand in the heavenly places, far above all rule, and authority, and power, and dominion, and every name that is named, not only in this world, but also in that which is to come: and he put all things in subjection under his feet, and gave him to be head over all things to the church, which is his body, the fulness of him that filleth all in all.

Shall we pray:

Beloved Lord, we have already been found in Your presence for some time expressing our worship, our praise, our thanksgiving, our love. And Lord, we have committed the ministry of Your word to You as well. All we want to do is recognize before You that we need that anointing, both for the speaking of Your word and the hearing of Your word. Dear Lord, we praise You that at great cost You have provided that anointing. Into it by faith we stand, that upon the speaking of Your word there will be such an anointing and upon the hearing of Your word there will also be such an anointing, that Your purpose and will in this time will be fulfilled. We shall be careful, Lord, to give You all the praise and worship of our hearts for answering this prayer of ours. In the name of our Messiah, the Lord Jesus. Amen.

We have been considering this testimony of the apostle Paul as it is recorded here in chapter 3 of the Philippian letter. The Bible is full of testimonies, but in my estimation there is no testimony more remarkable and in some ways more significant than this testimony of the apostle Paul. Apart from anything else it raises some very serious questions. I have pointed out those questions.

This is no ordinary testimony. Here is a man who has experienced so much of the Lord, whose knowledge of the Lord leaves all of us stunned really. Who has ever fully understood what the apostle has given us in Romans, in I and II Corinthians, in Ephesians, and in Colossians? There is a wealth here that no child of God has ever fully exhausted; it is so tremendous. Yet here he is speaking about the fact that he has not already obtained, he has not already been made perfect, he counts not himself yet to have laid hold. Where does that leave us? This apostle, this servant of God, this child of God, who has experienced so much, who has gone so far with the Lord, who has been given such tremendous revelations of the Lord, if he feels he has not yet laid hold, and if he feels he has not yet obtained, where does that leave you and me?

He speaks about a goal. He is not speaking about the possibility, in my estimation, of losing his salvation. He is speaking about a goal, the goal of God. Why has the Lord laid hold on us? For what cause has the Lord laid hold of us? He speaks of a goal and says, "I press on toward the goal to the prize of the high calling of God in Christ Jesus.

Here is a man who the more he sees of the Lord, the more he knows there is yet to see. The more he knows of the Lord, the more he knows there is to know of the Lord. It is as if he has been introduced to something so inexhaustible, so infinite, so endless, so eternal, so fathomless, it has inflamed his heart. This is no small gospel. This is no small Christ. This is something so tremendous that it spills out all these years later.

As we read this servant of God's testimony, something of it is still infectious. It inflames us; it infects us. As we listen to it, we wonder what it is that has caught this man that he cannot stand still. He has to forget the things which are behind. He has to stretch forward to the things which are before. What he has given us already is so tremendous, yet he speaks of pressing on.

I believe you receive the Lord Jesus as Savior. This is God's unconditional gift to you. It is all of grace. You receive Him as Savior, you receive Him as Redeemer, you receive Him as Deliverer, you receive Him as Life; but you win Him as Bridegroom. In my estimation that puts this whole testimony into perspective. You realize the apostle Paul is not saying he is going to win Christ as Bridegroom through works. What he is saying is this: unless we lay hold of the grace of God, unless we take hold of it, we shall not win Him as Bridegroom.

I asked the question: For what has the Lord laid hold of you? If you are born of God, if you are a child of God, then Christ has laid hold of you. You may not even realize it but Christ has laid hold of you. For what has He laid hold of you? I mentioned five things. The first was for glory, that you may share His glory, that you might come to His glory, that you may be glorified.

The second thing was that you may be changed into His likeness. That is amazing. For the more we go on with the Lord, the more unlike the Lord we see ourselves to be. But He has predestined us to be changed into the likeness of His Son. That is tremendous.

The third thing is that we might come to His throne and reign with Him, rule with Him in the throne. That requires training, education, discipline.

The fourth thing is that you might be His bride. We spoke about the love of God, and the fact that love always seeks for love. Without love we have nothing. We may have all knowledge, we may have all faith to remove mountains, we may understand the mysteries, we may even give our bodies to be burned, but the Book says, "Without love we are nothing." It all adds up to nothing. The last thing for which the Lord has laid hold on you is that you, with the Lord Jesus, might become the eternal home of God.

Pressing On

Now I want very simply to take up one last matter. It is also found in this verse 12: "Not that I have already obtained, or am already made perfect: but I press on, if so be that I may lay hold on that for which also I was laid hold on by Christ Jesus."

It is so simple but the practical key, the heart of the matter is whether you lay hold on that for which Christ has laid hold on you. I do not know what it is about Christian people, but they become (if I may put it this way) converted dummies, Christian couch potatoes. That means they sit on a couch and look at television, and that is exactly what thousands of Christians become. They go to church, they sit, as it were, on a couch, and they watch a kind of Christian television. It is all there. Someone is speaking. One person does it all, or two or three people do it all. They sit there like dummies, just taking it in. Of course it is easy to criticize: "I did not get anything out of that." "That was quite interesting, wasn't it?" "Did you hear the jokes that were made? Weren't they terrific?" It is just like dummies, couch potatoes.

They are not growing. They are not going on with the Lord. They are not pressing on. They are not getting anywhere. They are the same today as they were this time last year. They are the same today as they were five years ago, only a little older. That is the only difference. But there are tens of thousands, millions of Christians who are in this category.

It is all very well to talk about that for which Christ laid hold on you, but nothing will happen unless you lay hold on that for which He laid hold on you. I do not know how the Lord laid hold on you. There are so many ways that the Lord lays hold of us. Some of us went forward at a meeting, a crusade. Some of us stood up. I myself stood up. I hardly knew what I was doing. My sister was sitting next to me at the second Christian meeting that we had ever been in. I had a discussion with my sister who was ten;

I was twelve. And I said, "Should I stand up?" She said, "Never." Actually in the end she became a better believer than I, but she said, "You cannot do that." But I finally stood up.

A tremendous sense of sinfulness came to me even though I was only twelve. I wept and wept and wept. The old gentleman who came to help me put his arms around me and said, "What is it that you are weeping about?" When I said, "I am such a sinner," that old gentleman just looked at me. I am sure he wondered how I could be such a sinner at twelve. But I was saved that night. I have never forgotten another old gentleman, a pastor, who came up and said, "Young man, when you stood up, God said to me: 'Pray for this young man because I will use him.'" I never forgot the old boy. He was such an old gentleman. He looked as if he was Methuselah.

I remember one fellow who was a captain in the Merchant Navy. He was a blackguard, a drunkard. He used to come home to his wife and fall on the floor, sick and vomiting. He would lie there all night. One night he came in, fell on the floor and was sick. The next morning his wife, who had learned to leave him on the floor, came to him and he said, "Make me a cup of coffee." When she brought him the coffee, he said, "Have we got a Bible in this house?" And she said, "You are not going to make fun now of the Bible. You have made fun of everything else that is sacred. Are you going to make fun of it?" "No," he said, "I want to read it."

He got saved in a drunken stupor. What else could he be but a Calvinist? He never made a decision. Two weeks later his wife was sweeping the corridor. She stopped and leaned on the top of the broom and thought to herself: "What has happened to my husband? He stopped drinking, he stopped swearing, he is loving, he is kind, and he says he has found God." And she got saved, leaning on the top of a broom.

I do not know how you got saved. Whether you made a decision, whether you stood up, whether you went forward, whether you signed something, or whether in some amazing way the Lord just arrested you, what ever it was, it was the Lord who laid hold on you. You may not have even realized it but it was the Lord who arrested you. He apprehended you; He took hold of you.

I remember saying to the boys at school, some of whom were Christians and belonged to an organization called Crusaders. I used to make fun of them and say, "I do not believe that Jesus even existed. He is a legend, a myth." Can you imagine what happens when the Lord arrests you!

It is precisely the same word that the Spirit of God uses through the apostle Paul concerning you. You now have to apprehend that for which the Lord has apprehended you. You have to take hold of that for which the Lord Jesus has taken hold of you. If you do not, if you do not press on, if you do not move forward, if you do not by faith appropriate, you get nowhere. You join the great number of Christian couch potatoes, dummies, pew warmers, seat warmers. May the Lord help us.

Power to Lay Hold

There are three things about laying hold of the Lord that I want very simply to talk about. The first is that you need power to lay hold on that for which the Lord laid hold on you. It is so simple. The grace is there but you need power to take hold of that grace.

On my journey here from Los Angeles we were driven by a dear brother to a certain place on the outskirts of L.A. We transferred cars to a very dear sister who was going to bring us the rest of the way. We had a very interesting meal in a very interesting place and then the brother who brought us left and we got into the car. When she turned the ignition, nothing happened. Her face was a picture. "Well," she said, looking at me, "this has never happened before." So she turned it again. No power. Then she did something underneath and turned it again. No power. We had a car, we had provisions, we had our luggage, there was the three of us, we were on the right road and, we had the address where we were going. We even had gas in the car, but we had no power. Across the road there was a Barnes & Noble and she said, "You go over there and stay for a while." I stayed there for an hour and when I finally came out some very kind gentleman from an automobile association had come and he did something to the car. We never had any more problems at all.

Many of you are just like that car, just like we were. Everything is there. You have the map, you have the address, you know where you are going, you have the car, you have the provisions, you even have the gas, but there is no power. To lay hold on that for which Christ has laid hold on you requires power. The apostle Paul in his testimony said, "That I may know Him and the power of His resurrection." There is something about resurrection life. It is doing the impossible. Death is the final thing, isn't it?

There is a famous baseball player that you all probably know. I do not know anything about baseball. I only noticed it was on the news every day. It did not matter if half the world was dying elsewhere. It was all about this baseball player and the argument in his family about deep-freezing him. The gentleman who founded this deep freezing business also came on television, and he looked as if he had been frozen. He was terrible looking.

What a mess all of this is! I heard this man, who looked like death not even warmed up, saying, "You know, there is no such thing as death. If we can keep them deep frozen there will come a day when we can unfreeze them." God help us.

"The power of His resurrection." Resurrection is the other side of death. Death is final. You cannot do anything about death. When a person is still breathing, you can do something, but once they are dead it is over. This is power that is on the other side. It is a life that has triumphed over death, a life that breaks through every problem and triumphs over every obstacle and brings about the fulfillment of the purpose of God.

Jesus said, "I am the resurrection and the life." It is not just something that lies ahead, but it is the power of His resurrection that you and I can know now. The apostle Paul put it very clearly in II Corinthians 1:8–9: "For we would not have you ignorant, brethren, concerning our affliction which befell us in Asia, that we were weighed down exceedingly, beyond our power, insomuch that we despaired even of life: yea, we ourselves have had the sentence of death within ourselves, that we should not trust in ourselves, but in God who raiseth the dead."

What kind of experience did Paul and his co-workers have that they felt they were weighed down so they even despaired of life? They could only say, "We had the sentence of death within ourselves." He sees it as education, as training. He says that we should not trust in ourselves but in God who raises the dead. "That I might know Him and the power of His resurrection."

His Power to Usward Who Believe

In Ephesians the apostle prays for three things. He prays for those who read this letter that the eyes of their hearts might be enlightened and the spirit of wisdom and revelation should be given to them in the knowledge of the Lord Jesus. This is given in order that they might know, not about, but they might know what is the hope of His calling, what the riches of the glory of His inheritance is in the saints, and what is the exceeding greatness of His power to usward who believe. One version translates it like this: "The surpassing greatness of His power which He wrought in Christ Jesus when He raised Him from the dead." Not only did He raise Him from the dead but He made Him to sit far above all rule and power and authority. Then it says, "He placed all things in subjection under His feet and gave Him to be head over all things to the church which is His body."

In other words, if you are in Christ, you are between the Head, Christ who is Head over everything, and the feet, all things are in subjection under His feet. Tremendous! That means there is no obstacle the Lord cannot overcome. There is nothing the Lord cannot do. There is no difficulty that the Lord cannot solve. There is nothing impossible with the Lord. Now, the Lord does not always do everything because in leaving things we are trained, educated, disciplined.

There are times when the Lord steps into your life and in a single moment it has all happened. You are left stunned. "Why," you say, "look at what the Lord has done." The mountains have melted down at His presence. He just came in and this huge mountain of difficulty, this obstacle, this thing that seemed so impossible, disappeared." Surely you all must have had such an experience some time or another.

There are other times when the Lord leaves the mountain and you stare at it, and stare at it, and stare at it. The only way that mountain is moved is when you have God-given faith to move it. Then you have to speak the word over it. It is not the greatness of your faith; it is the greatness of your Lord. Faith never removes mountains. It is God who removes mountains, but faith, even as small as a grain of mustard seed in you, once it functions, once it operates, joins you to the infinity of God. Then the mountain is moved.

There is yet another way the Lord deals with mountains. He gives you hinds' feet. He leaves the mountain and says, "You are going to live in it." Many believers have elephants' feet. They are not adapted for such mountains. You have to have hinds' feet.

Have you ever seen hinds? Have you ever seen an antelope, or ibex? He jumps in high places, from one ledge to another, unfailingly. Now and again I have seen one fall but very, very rarely. If one falls it is usually because it is sick. But normally they have feet adapted for impossible places.

Could you believe that you could live in such impossible places? The surpassing greatness of this power to usward who believe is for you. It is not just for the elite saint; it is for you, whoever you are—if you believe. Do you believe? Are you a believer, someone who Christ has laid hold of? This exceeding greatness of His power, the same power that brought Jesus out of the tomb when the whole of hell was mobilized to keep Him in, is yours. It is to usward who believe. Whether He causes the mountain to melt and you do nothing, or whether you have to see the greatness of the Lord and faith is born in your heart so that you can speak the word to the mountain and the mountain moves, or whether you learn to live in the mountain with hinds' feet, you press on.

We need such power. Do you have this power? It is yours. Are you a believer? Do you think the Lord Jesus has left you to find your own way? Do you look at the mountain and say, "Oh, poor me, poor me? Why do I have mountain range after mountain range after mountain range?" The Lord is training you. The Lord is educating you. The Lord is increasing your capacity for glory. The Lord is changing you into His likeness. It is all part of the school of Christ.

The Eternal Agent

Why are we so afraid of the Holy Spirit? It is extraordinary to me that believers are so often afraid when we start to talk about the Holy Spirit and they say, "Be careful, be careful. God forbid, we might become Pentecostals. Worse still, we might even become Charismatics. We must be careful." The word is very, very clear. Jesus said to them: "Wait in Jerusalem until you are clothed with power from on high." How can you and I know the power of His resurrection apart from the Holy Spirit? How can we know the surpassing greatness of His power which He wrought in Christ when He raised Him from the dead? Who raised Jesus from the dead?

In Romans 8 it says, "The Spirit of Him who raised Jesus from the dead." It is the Spirit of God. He raised Jesus from the dead. Sometimes we speak of theology in a rather poor way because often it brings so much death. But we cannot do without true theology. Everything originates in God the Father, and through the Son He does everything, and for the Son He does everything. The Holy Spirit is the eternal Agent. He is the Supervisor of the whole practical work of God. You cannot devalue the Holy Spirit. You cannot by-pass the Holy Spirit. You cannot talk about the Lord Jesus as if the Holy Spirit does not matter, because the Lord Jesus said that He would not leave us orphans but would come to us. And He spoke about the gift of the Holy Spirit.

I believe this is of tremendous importance for all of us. It is not that we want you to have some experience of the Holy Spirit that you will trap within yourself and become sort of very proud about it and say, "Yes, I have the Holy Spirit. I have had an experience of the Holy Spirit." What we want is that the Holy Spirit will get you. When the Holy Spirit gets you, you will discover that you are lost in the beauty of the Lord Jesus, lost in the fulness of God in the Lord Jesus, and lost in the unsearchable riches of the Lord Jesus. It is the work of the Holy Spirit. It is the Holy Spirit who unveils the Lord Jesus to us. It is the Holy Spirit who turns our heart to see Him, even in tribulation and affliction. It is the Holy Spirit who unites us with God in Christ. It is the Holy Spirit who takes of the things of the Lord Jesus and makes them real to us.

Clothed with Power

"Clothed with power from on high." When you are properly clothed, you are not self-conscious. You do not paint a house or change the oil in the car in a tuxedo. Ladies do not clean the house in their best dress. You do not dress up beautifully to cook a meal for fourteen people. Whatever job it is requires certain clothing, and when you have the right clothing, you are not self-conscious.

You are only conscious of the job you have to do. But when you are wearing the wrong clothing, you are very self-conscious. Am I dressed for this?

I always remember something that happened years ago in Richmond, Surrey, England. We had a gospel meeting every Sunday evening. In those days so many folks came in from the street and found the Lord. On this occasion I was to preach that evening, and I don't know how it happened but I went all the way from the family home, which was on the other side of the River Thames over a little lake, and then over the old Richmond bridge until I came to Halford House. I went in the back garden gate through the garden to the house.

The brothers always used to meet together to pray for the meeting, the actual gospel meeting, and the preaching of the word. As we gathered around to pray in the library, one of the brothers was praying, and I had my head down. I opened my eyes and I said, "Ohhh!"

They all stopped praying. For a minute I think they thought I had expired, that I had had a heart attack. They said, "What is wrong?"

And I said, "Look, I have bright red slippers on."

Now I know in California you can wear anything but not in England. So they said, "Brother, don't worry about it. Nobody will see them."

"No," I said, "I cannot preach with those red slippers."

And they said, "When you stand behind the table, nobody will see the red slippers."

I said, "I cannot do it. When I walk from the chair up there, I am sure they will all go 'ahhh!' While I am preaching, if someone holds their head in their hand, I will think they are thinking, 'What kind of brother is this?' If some sister bows her head to pray, I will think instantly that she is saying, 'Dear Lord, forgive him.'"

Then one of the brothers said, "Okay, I have my bike here. I will cycle back over to your home and get your shoes." In twenty minutes he was back with the shoes. I put the shoes on and I never thought about my feet again. When I preached that night, I was only conscious of the message God had given me and the unsaved people that were present. That was all I thought about, whereas with my red slippers I would have continually thought of them. While I was preaching the gospel, if I saw anyone bow their head I would have thought they had seen my slippers.

"Clothed with power from on high." When the Holy Spirit clothes you with power from on high, you can get on with the job. You are not self-conscious. You are only conscious of what the Lord is saying to you and what He is giving to you to do.

"If so be that I may lay hold on that for which also I was laid hold on by Christ Jesus." Power! We need such power to lay hold of the grace, to lay hold of the anointing, to stand for the Lord and with the Lord. We need such power to be a witness, power to do the work of the Lord. We need such power.

The Obstacle to Laying Hold

The second thing is very simple as well. Every single one of us has an obstacle to laying hold on that for which Christ has laid hold of us. What is that obstacle? The greatest problem we have is not a question of vision. Vision is necessary but it is not just a question of vision or of understanding. The problem is self. It is the biggest obstacle to laying hold on that for which Christ has laid hold of you. We think: "Will it cost me my self-life? I would rather not lay hold on. I would rather just coast along."

We all are so deceitful. We always think: "Later." You younger ones think, "I am only young once. Why not enjoy myself when I am young?" There is nothing wrong in enjoying yourself but where did all that come from? It comes from a self-life.

Let me put it another way. It says in Mark 8:31–33: "And [Jesus] began to teach them, that the Son of man must suffer many things, and be rejected by the elders, and the chief priests, and the scribes, and be killed, and after three days rise again. And he spake the saying openly. And Peter took him, and began to rebuke him. But he turning about, and seeing his disciples, rebuked Peter, and saith, Get thee behind me, Satan; for thou mindest not the things of God, but the things of men."

How could the Lord have been so unkind? Peter was horrified at the thought that Jesus was going to go through a crucifixion, and even if Jesus spoke about being raised on the third day, the whole thing was anathema to Peter. "How could You speak about such a thing?" he said. "Lord, this is not right. I will not allow it." Peter was a big burly fellow. He was not afraid of saying what he thought. Jesus looked into his eyes and said, "Get behind Me, Satan."

"Well, I think that is terrible," Peter could have said. "Did I hear aright? Did You say to me 'Get behind Me, Satan,' as You looked into my eyes? You are not looking behind me."

"Leave him alone, Satan"; that would have been right. Or if he had said to him, "Satan is troubling your mind, Peter"; that would have been okay. Or if he had said better still, "You are thinking negative thoughts." But instead, looking into Peter's eyes he said, "Get behind Me, Satan. You do not mind the things of God. You mind the things of man."

Your self-life always minds the things of man, even when it is Christianized. It is always interested in self—its fulfillment, its satisfaction, its joy, its will, its progress. It always minds the things of man, not the things of God.

Dear brother, dear sister, your uncrucified self-life is satanized. I say it again; it is satanized. By the fall of man a terrible change took place in our human constitution and self became a little demi, mini god. I, I, I; everything is I. It begins with I; it ends with I. Sin is s-I-n. Sins come out of the I life. It is satanized.

Eve listened to the serpent when he said to her, "Did God say you would die? You will not die. He knows you will become as God." There was a little bit of truth in what he said. "You will be able to live independently of God, you will be able to live self-sufficiently, you will spend your whole life, as it were, training your self-life." This is world history. The whole of the history of the world is summed up in this satanized self-life.

You do not have to listen to me, but if you want to press on with the Lord, you will have to face your satanized self-life. It will get you out of the will of God even when it is Christianized. Oh, we have done a tremendous job with this old self-life of ours. We have Christianized it, taught it Christian phraseology. Oh, what a mess we have made in the work of God and in the church of God.

The Self-Life Under New Management

Of course, there is a self-life, but it is a different kind of self-life. If I may put it very simply, it is under another management. When you lose your life—the word in Greek is psuche, which is your soul life—for His sake and the gospel, you save it. You have found it unto life eternal. But when you hold onto it, hug it, dress it up as a good Christian, you lose it. It is like manna kept too long. The worms come out.

You young people, your self-life will bring you to the wrong husband, to the wrong wife, to the wrong job, to the wrong experiences. Then, when you are corrupted and when you have lost nearly everything, you will turn to the Lord. It is a sad thing that sometimes the only way we can learn is to go the wrong way. It is not necessary. Our Lord Jesus said, "If any man come after Me, let him deny himself, take up his cross, and follow Me." Take up his cross! It was the crossbeam, not the upright. Take up his cross? Yes, you will not get crucified. You have got the sentence of death. Others will crucify you.

The apostle Paul said in Galatians 2:20: "I have been crucified with Christ; nevertheless I live, yet not I but Christ liveth in me: and the life which I now live I live by the faith of the Son of God, who loved me and gave Himself for me." "I have been crucified with Christ." That means when Christ was crucified, I was crucified. I do not know of any better illustration than the one I was taught and it helped me so much. Think of these notes as you and this Bible as Christ. God put you in Christ. If I put these notes in my Bible, you cannot see them. They are in the Bible. If I put the Bible on the table, where are the notes? They are in the Bible. If I put the Bible on the piano, where are the notes?

The notes are on the piano but I cannot see them. Wherever the Bible goes the notes go. The history of the Bible is the history of the notes. When God crucified the Lord Jesus, He knew you from the beginning, and you were in Christ. So when Christ was crucified, He not only died for you He died as you.

Some people say you must have this first before you know the power of the Holy Spirit, but in my estimation you will never really know the cross unless you have the power of the Holy Spirit. Many a person has had an experience of the Holy Spirit which evaporated within days, months, a year or two. Why? It is because they never learned this lesson of the cross. When a life is laid down, there is an open heaven. When a life is laid down, the anointing is available. When a life is laid down, all the power of God is provided.

The Secret of Dying

Until we are prepared to lose our self-life, lay it down, deny ourselves, take up our cross, there can be no laying hold on that for which Christ laid hold of you. Everywhere I go I am asked, especially by young people: "How can we live the Christian life?" This is not the problem. You say, "Not the problem? We have been listening to you for a while and we would have thought the problem is living the Christian life. We are not really living it. How can we live it?" It is not the problem. The problem is how to die. If once you have the secret of dying, the life will take care of itself. Once you know how to fall into the ground and die, there will be a harvest. Once you lose your life you will save it. It will be given back under new management.

The problem is how to die. Have you got a difficult parent? Die. Have you got a difficult husband? Die. Have you got a difficult wife? Die. Do you have difficult children? Die. Do you have a difficult boss? Die. Do you have difficult employees? Die. Once you learn how to die, the life of God is spontaneous. You walk in newness of life. You are no longer a statue, a dummy, a couch potato. You are walking; you are pressing on; you are moving. Something has happened.

I am often asked: "How can we live church life?" The problem is not how to live church life with all its complexities, difficulties, and obstacles. The problem is how to die. Once we learn how to die, church life is spontaneous. When you get two or three people who all know how to die, you have church life. Otherwise, it is I, I, I. I feel; I know; I think; it is my opinion. Oh, don't we all know it? Church life is like guns turned on one another. It is like one of those Mafia gunfights. They were all buddies once; now they are turning the guns on one another. Isn't this the history of the church?

Grace Through Faith

The third thing I want to say is that it is all by grace through faith. Could there be anything more simple? It is all by grace through faith. It is faith, living faith; not dead academic faith. It is living faith that lays hold on that for which Christ laid hold on you.

It is in Ephesians 2:8: "By grace have you been saved through faith; and that not of yourself, it is the gift of God." How can you lay hold on that for which Christ laid hold on you? It is: "By grace through faith."

In Colossians 2:6–7 the apostle says, "As therefore ye received Christ Jesus the Lord, so walk in him, rooted and builded up in him, and established in your faith, even as ye were taught, abounding in thanksgiving."

What is the key to this? As you received Christ Jesus, so walk in Him. How did you receive the Lord Jesus? It was by the grace of God through faith, which is the gift of God. How do you take further steps? It is by grace through faith. Every step in this walk, every step is by grace through faith.

Running is only walking, speeded up. I sometimes get the impression when I read and hear the testimony of the apostle Paul that he is in a great race. He is not going to slow down. He is not going to turn to the left or to the right. He is straight ahead. He is not going to look back. He is stretching forward to what is before. He is pressing on to win the prize.

How can you press on? It will be by grace through faith. May God touch every one of our hearts and lives. The Lord Jesus has laid hold of us but we have to lay hold on that for which He also laid hold on us.

Shall we pray:

Beloved Lord, we need to lay hold on that for which You have laid hold on us. It is tremendous, Lord, that you have taken hold of us, and brought us into Your salvation. Will You challenge us? Where there is no power, bring us into a knowing of the power of Your resurrection by the Spirit of God. Where we feel we have obstacles and problems and difficulties that are so enormous, help us to see that it is the surpassing greatness of Your power that is to usward who believe.

Touch us, Lord. Open our eyes to Your greatness, to Your power, that with You nothing is impossible and nothing too hard. And where there is a self-life, a satanized self-life, molly-coddled, seeking its fulfillment, its satisfaction, oh beloved Lord, help us. Help us by that power of Your Spirit to lose it, to let go of it, to deny ourselves and take up that crossbeam and follow You.

Hear us, Lord. Let Your grace be manifest in every one of our lives and stir up the grain of mustard seed faith in every one of us to take hold of that for which You have taken hold of us. We want to come to the goal. We want to win the prize. We want to be part of that capital city. We want to be part of that bride, that home of Yours. Lord, work in us we pray by Your Holy Spirit. We ask it in the name of our Lord Jesus. Amen.

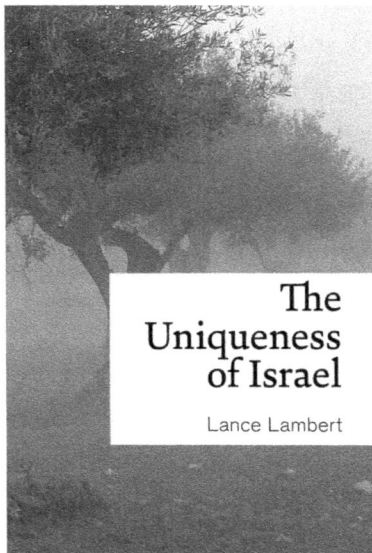

The Uniqueness of Israel

Woven into the fabric of Jewish existence there is an undeniable uniqueness. There is bitter controversy over the subject of Israel, but time itself will establish the truth about this nation's place in God's plan. For Lance Lambert, the Lord Jesus is the key that unlocks Jewish history He is the key not only to their fall, but also to their restoration. For in spite of the fact that they rejected Him, He has not rejected them.

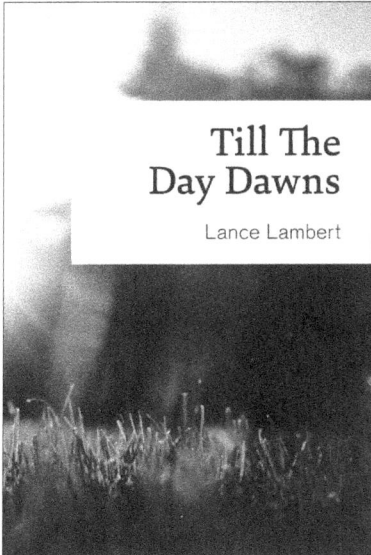

Till the Day Dawns

"And we have the word of prophecy made more sure; whereunto ye do well that ye take heed, as unto a lamp shining in a dark place, until the day dawn, and the day-star arise in your hearts." (II Peter 1:9).

The word of prophecy was not given that we might merely be comforted but that we would be prepared and made ready. Let us look into the Word of God together, searching out the prophecies, that the Day-Star arise in our hearts until the Day dawns.

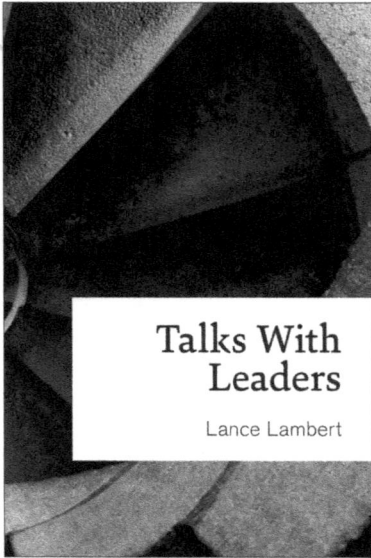

Talks With Leaders

Talks With
Leaders

Lance Lambert

Talks With Leaders

"O Timothy, guard that which is committed unto thee ..."
(1 Timothy 6:20) Has God given you something? Has God
deposited something in you? Is there something of Himself
which He has given to you to contribute to the people of God?
Guard it. Guard that vision which He has given you. Guard that
understanding that He has so mercifully granted to you. Guard
that experience which He has given that it does not evaporate or
drain away or become a cause of pride. Guard that which the Lord
has given to you by the Holy Spirit. In these heart-to-heart talks
with leaders Lance Lambert covers such topics as the character
of God's servants, the way to serve, the importance of anointing,
and hearing God's voice. Let us consider together how to remain
faithful with what has been entrusted to us.

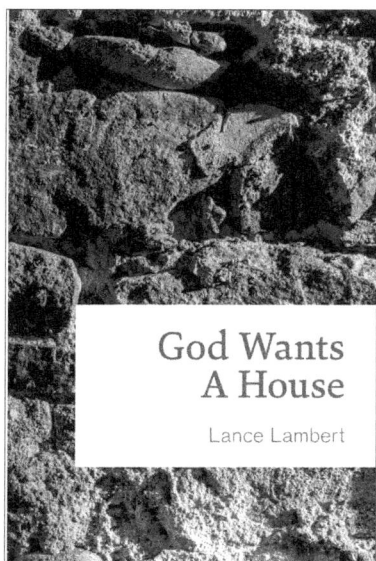

God Wants a House

Where is God at home? Is He at home in Richmond, VA? Is He at home in Washington? Is He at home in Richmond, Surrey? Is He at home in these other places? Where is God at home? There are thousands of living stones, many, many dear believers with real experience of the Lord, but where has the ark come home? Where are the staves being lengthened that God has finally come home? In God Wants a House Lance looks into this desire of the Lord, this desire He has to dwell with His people. What would this dwelling look like? Let's seek the Lord, that we can say with David, "One thing have I asked of Jehovah, that will I seek after: that I may dwell in the house of Jehovah all the days of my life, To behold the beauty of Jehovah, And to inquire in his temple."